Walking London's History

2000 YEARS IN 15 WALKS

TIM POTTER

First published: July 2020

ISBN No: 979-8-662667-44-0

Maps by Alan Boyd

Typesetting by David Siddall Multimedia, Dartmouth, UK
www.davidsiddall.com

Contents

Introduction v

Roman London 1

Medieval London 13

Reformation London..23

The Great Fire of London 32

Greenwich: Wren's Vision for London....................................42

Doctor Johnson's London 52

London's Docks 64

       Wapping...66

       Wapping to Canary Wharf 76

Regency London 84

The highpoint of Victorian London – Albertopolis 96

The other side of Victorian London – the East End..............108

Victorian philanthropy in Whitechapel and Stepney 121

Literary London and the Bloomsbury Set............................134

Twenty-first Century London 147

Two thousand years of history 155

A big thank you to all those who helped with this book by coming on the walks, reading early drafts and making suggestions.

To Alan for the maps and, most of all, to my family for putting up with me.

Introduction

London is a profoundly modern city. But one with a long history. Today it is a global metropolis fit for the twenty first century but it is founded on two thousand years of history. The streets of central London are full of tantalising glimpses of the past, yet few Londoners know very much about their city's history. Indeed many who have lived and worked in the city for decades know less about it than a tourist who comes for a fortnight armed with a good guidebook.

My aim is to explore London's history over the last two thousand years through fifteen short walks, most through the heart of the City. I start with the Romans and end with the architecture of the twenty first century. As you follow the walks, so you will understand a lot more about the history of London over the last two millennia. Each walk in this book explores a particular period of London's history. The route is set in its historical context by a brief summary of the time and the main themes which characterised the City's development. This will help you understand what you are seeing when you go walking and how it fits into the story of London.

The walks in this book are based on tours round London that I have developed over the last few years. They are mainly quite short, only a couple of miles, but they're so interesting that each one normally takes about two hours.

The walks don't visit every significant site in London. When we cover the medieval period, for instance, we leave out the three great London buildings of that era: Westminster Abbey, the Tower of London and Southwark Cathedral. These are all wonderful but they are on every London tourist trail. Instead I will take you through the lesser known medieval sites of London; the ones the tourists don't visit. These walks will try and keep you away from the crowds to discover the hidden corners of London which are much quieter but spectacular none the less. Sometimes we will be walking in the footsteps of great writers and poets who have made London their home. Pepys, Dickens, Shakespeare, Dr. Johnson and Virginia Woolf all make an appearance here. More often though we will be trying to recreate the lives of ordinary Londoners and the great events they lived through. While each of the routes has been designed to focus on a particular era in London's history, when we pass wonderful spots from other centuries they are, of course, highlighted and their significance explained. If you complete all of these walks I can promise that you will learn a great deal about London and its history as well as the lives of Londoners over the centuries. You will also see some of the finest sights the City has to offer.

For me these walks reveal everything that is great about London. The beautiful views, the unexplored corners and tiny alleys, the knowledge that every time you walk you will see something new and learn something remarkable. Above all I hope I can share with you that haunting sense of the past which for me pervades so much of this great city.

Tim Potter

Roman London

London is still at its very heart a Roman city. The Romans chose the site, named it, developed its first road system, fixed its boundaries and turned it into the most important city in Britain. To understand modern London you need to understand its foundation.

The Britain that Rome conquered was not a blank page to be written on. Pre-Roman Britain had a surprisingly advanced culture. It had traded with the Phoenicians from what is now Lebanon for 800 years and imported goods from all over Europe. The people, based in loose tribal groups, produced some beautiful artefacts but they were no match for the might of the Roman Empire.

Britain was seen by the Romans as the very edge of the world, the place where dead souls migrated to. Indeed, the Isle of Thanet where the Romans first arrived takes its name from Thanatos, the Greek God of death, which some may feel is a bit harsh on the people of Ramsgate.

Julius Caesar paid two flying visits in 55 and 54 BC, where he claimed Britain as part of the Roman Empire. Whilst he 'Veni, Vidi, Vinci', (he came, he saw, he conquered), he didn't stay and Britain remained outside the Empire. The Roman occupation proper began almost one hundred years later when, in 43AD, Claudius sent four legions to invade Britain. They made steady progress conquering the whole of southern and eastern England within a few years. The key geographical feature of Southern Britain, the Thames, was both a challenge and an opportunity for the Romans: the river was a significant barrier which needed a permanent crossing point but it could also serve as an easy supply route for both men and materials from the continent.

The Thames in Roman times was very different from the river we see today. It was more like a lake than a river, probably three times wider than it is today. Consequently, the current was slower, the tides were weaker and it was much shallower. The original crossing of the Thames seems to have been at a ford in what is now Westminster but there was a much better site than that low lying, muddy marsh. Just a couple of miles downstream the swamp gave way to three small hills on the north bank; today we call them Ludgate Hill, Corn Hill and Tower Hill. Crucially, at that point the river was shallow and narrow enough for a bridge to be built to span the Thames. Once the bridge was built, a garrison with a settlement was needed to protect it. And so London, or Londinium as the Romans named it, was born.

It proved to be a great site for a city. The river was still tidal helping boats to reach the city's wharves against the prevailing winds and current. There was safe anchorage in the Walbrook and River Fleet and the three hills provided a drier environment for the newly founded township. Within ten years it seems that Londinium was booming, attracting citizens from all over the Roman Empire as well as native Britons from the south of England. Centred initially on the banks of the Walbrook, it became a trading centre for the new province, importing stone, timber, exotic new foodstuffs, wine and oil. In return, the city exported grain, precious metals and slaves. But its development was certainly anything but smooth.

Around 60 AD, the Iceni, a tribe from East Anglia rose up against the severity of Roman rule. Led by their queen, Boudicca, they first destroyed Camulodunum (Colchester), the original capital of Roman Britain, and then her forces marched on Londinium. The Roman military commander, Suetonius, outnumbered by the rebels abandoned the city to its fate. Boudica was merciless, torturing and killing every inhabitant left in Londinium and burning the city to the ground. She then moved on to Verulamium (St. Albans) where she massacred its population.

The devastation was total. Archaeologists have discovered a layer of ash underneath London's streets dating back to the rebellion. More macabre has been the discovery of Roman era skulls in the Walbrook which some believe to have been the result of the rebellion. According to Tacitus, over 70,000 civilians, Roman and British, died in the three towns. It seems that Boudicca probably killed more Londoners than any other single person in history, more than Hitler during the Blitz. Yet somehow over the years this rebel queen became a heroine of the city whose statue now stands on Westminster Bridge defending the city she once destroyed.

Londinium's recovery from Boudicca's rebellion was swift. Within the space of ten years the city was booming once again. Roads were constructed linking London with the rest of the province. Great public buildings were created: baths at Billingsgate, a forum at Leadenhall, an amphitheatre at the Guildhall, a temple to Mithras on the banks of the Walbrook, the governor's palace now buried by Cannon Street station. Most impressively, a great wall was built around Londinium in around 200AD including along the river front to protect the City from attack. The wall demarcated much of the City of London's boundaries that have lasted, almost unchanged, till the present day.

At its height in the middle of the second century, Londinium was one of the greatest Roman cities outside Italy with perhaps 60,000 inhabitants. Her citizens came from all over Britain and Europe including what is now Spain, France and Africa. From its very creation, London has been a multi-cultural city attracting migrants from the rest of Britain and abroad. Its forum, walls and amphitheatre were the match of any city north of the Alps and the city was a great trading centre. The forum, in particular, was enormous, a square with sides of some 168 metres long. It now lies hidden beneath Leadenhall Market.

But Roman power in Britain was not long lasting. Attacks in the border regions in Europe and Asia stretched Roman resources to breaking point. Successive emperors had neither the means nor the will to defend their far-flung provinces. Internal conflicts and rebellions in Britain threw the province into chaos hastening the end of Roman rule. By 400AD the whole Roman Empire was in crisis as its borders began to crumble and gradually Britain slipped out of Rome's control. The legions were recalled in 410AD from Britain never to be replaced and the governor's centralised power based in London came to an end.

While aspects of Roman culture persisted in England perhaps for another century, waves of Anglo-Saxon migrants began arriving in southern England and settling in the countryside. The nearest settlement was around Covent Garden but from the middle of the fifth century to 880AD, the London that Rome had built was deserted, an uninhabited ruin.

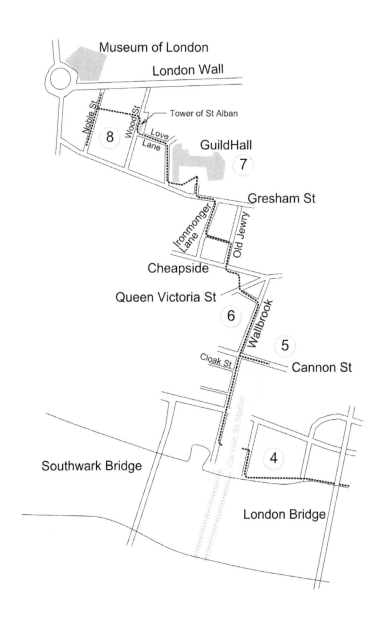

A walk through Roman London

This walk of around 2 miles takes in most of the main sites of Roman London which still exist today as we walk diagonally across the modern City.

1 Tower Hill Station (Start)

2 All Hallows Church

3 St Magnus the Martyr

4 Hanseatic League

5 London Stone

6 Temple of Mithras

7 Guildhall

8 Roman Wall

Details of what you'll see on this walk start on the next page...

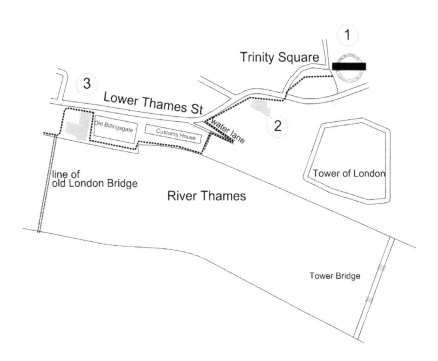

A Walk through Roman London: Stop 1

Come out of Tower Hill Station. Running along the east edge of the station is one of the best preserved sections of the old Roman wall. This was built sometime at the end of the second century, and later extended along the river bank to protect Londinium from attack from the river.

It is unclear as to exactly why the wall was built. Some believe there may have been an external threat to the City, necessitating a strong defence barrier but equally it may have been an attempt to make the city more prestigious. The original wall was some six metres high and protected by a two metre deep ditch. The part of the wall you're looking at clearly shows the original Roman wall and then its medieval repairs and extensions. Lines of characteristic red Roman tiles separate the finely cut Kentish ragstone blocks built by the Roman masons from the much poorer quality medieval wall.

Look towards the Tower of London and you will see a statue of a Roman Emperor standing in front of the wall. This is now purported to be Trajan but for some years it was believed it might be an early Roman governor. Much about the statue is unclear. The statue itself was found in a rubbish tip in Southampton, the head does not match the body and Trajan never visited Britain. Never mind; it's an impressive reminder of London's Roman roots.

Walk away from the wall and into Trinity Square aiming for the church across the road on the left hand corner of the square. You are now walking over Londinium. Ten metres under your feet are the remains of a major Roman structure faced with black marble built around 380. Its structure resembles a very ancient Roman cathedral in Milan and it could well be the first Christian church in London.

As you walk across Trinity Square, you are also at the centre of Britain's maritime history. Trinity House is on your right, the old Port of London Authority building is in the right hand corner and to your left, there are memorials to the dead of the merchant marine in the first and second world wars.

Ahead of you is one of the oldest and most famous churches in London – All Hallows by the Tower. This is our next stop.

Stop 2

All Hallows is one of the most ancient churches in London dating back to 675AD. Originally founded by the Saxons, it has been a witness to some of London's most tumultuous episodes. It was into this church that the body of Sir Thomas More was carried after his execution by Henry VIII on Tower Hill. All Hallows has been knocked about a bit over the last 1300 years; gunpowder barrels stored in the graveyard exploded in the Civil War and it narrowly escaped being destroyed by the Great Fire. Indeed up until the Blitz, scorch marks from the Fire could still be seen on its walls. It was badly damaged in the Blitz but beautifully restored and today it remains one of London's greatest churches.

There is much to see in the church and it repays a careful visit. There is a beautiful font cover carved by Grinling Gibbons, fine Tudor funerary monuments, sixteenth century brasses, a wonderful renaissance altarpiece and a Saxon arch which recycles old Roman tiles. But we are mainly interested in pre-Christian times and that means we must descend because Roman London is beneath our feet.

Just by the main entrance to the church, steep stairs descend to the crypt which now hosts an extraordinary collection of artefacts. As you enter the crypt you see a Roman pavement complete with original tesserae. There is also a plan of Roman London which, while a bit out of date due to new discoveries, gives a good visual reminder of the scale of Roman London. We will be walking across the city to the north west corner.

It is very worthwhile exploring the rest of the crypt. In the parish registers you can see the records of the baptism of William Penn, founder of Pennsylvania, the marriage of John Quincy Adams, the sixth president of the United States, and the burial certificate of Archbishop Laud, executed by Parliament during the Civil War. There is a succession of tiny medieval chapels, containing all kinds of exhibits such as an altar from Richard the Lionheart's Crusader castle of Athlit and the crow's nest of Shackleton's ship, The Endurance. Above all, just take a moment to imbibe the atmosphere; it's a truly wonderful place steeped in history.

Come out of the church and walk towards Lower Thames Street. You can see that the ground slopes away before you. Lower Thames Street is built on the site of the original Roman river bank. Since then the river has been progressively embanked narrowing the Thames. This has made the river far more powerful, the tides higher and the current much stronger than in Roman times.

Go down the steps, cross over Tower Place and then down Water Lane to the river. Walk along the Embankment in front of Custom House to Billingsgate.

Stop 3

You are rewarded with beautiful views of the south bank from Tower Bridge to London Bridge. The north east corner of Billingsgate conceals another monument to London's past; a Roman house complete with its own set of baths. Located at 101 Lower Thames Street, unfortunately it's open only on Saturdays with a pre-booked tour through the Museum of London.

Carry on walking towards London Bridge. Cut through the passage by the side of the blue glass building and turn left along Lower Thames Street. Fifty metres on and you are standing in the churchyard of St Magnus the Martyr.

Stop 4

This is almost certainly the site of the original Roman bridge. There are three clues: The structure you're standing in is the entrance to the medieval bridge which is likely to have used the original Roman foundations. The street facing you across the busy road, Fish Street Hill, is almost certainly a Roman road as it leads directly from the bridge to the remains of the Roman forum and then on to Bishopsgate and the north. Finally under the arch, you'll notice an iron-hard timber which once was part of the Roman wharf but used to be thought of as part of the original bridge.

The church is also well worth a visit. This was the first church to be destroyed in the Great Fire of London. Rebuilt by Christopher Wren, it is dedicated to Magnus Erlendsson, earl of Orkney. Inside the church there is an extraordinary statue of the martyred saint, complete with a historically inaccurate horned helmet. More important perhaps there is a famous model of the medieval London Bridge and, remarkably, a seventeenth century fire engine which we'll revisit on our Great Fire walk.

Retrace your steps back on to the river bank and walk under the new London Bridge built in 1973. The bridge it replaced of 1831 now resides proudly in the desert of Arizona. (It is an urban myth that the American buyer thought he was buying Tower Bridge!) Along the way and over the river you will see Southwark Cathedral, a replica of Drake's ship, the Golden Hind, and an awful lot of tourists.

Our river path ends at Allhallows Lane in front of the bridge taking trains into Cannon Street station. A plaque on the wall commemorates the history of the Hanseatic League which was based close to where you are now standing. The League were Baltic traders who formed a community here for more than 700 years from the twelfth century onwards on the banks of the Thames. They had their own gated community with warehouses, guildhall and accommodation. One of their specialities was the import of fur and we will see its legacy very shortly.

Walk under the railway lines following the illuminated pathway and turn right into Cousin Lane. You are now in the valley of the Walbrook, the ancient heart of Roman London. The stream provided a safer mooring for ships and boats and it was on its banks that the first settlement was founded.

Cross New Thames Street and continue walking up Dowgate Hill. On your left you will notice three of the Livery Halls which used to control trade and manufacturing in London up until the nineteenth century. They are the Skinners, the Dyers and the Tallow Chandlers Halls. This is what happened to the prized imports of the Hanseatic

League where sable and mink were skinned, dyed and then reduced to candles. Indeed, Cannon Street is a corruption of Candlewick Street because it once specialised in making candles.

As you walk up to Cannon Street a small road, Cloak Lane, is on your left. While this conjures up images of medieval knights its origins are much less salubrious. Cloak Lane is a corruption of Cloaca, Latin for sewer.

Turn right pass the entrance to Cannon Street Station. The station is built over the foundations of a major Roman palace, thought to be that of the Provincial Governor. In fact, where you are standing was probably the centre of Roman power in Britain.

Stop 5

Walk up Cannon Street to No. 111 on your left. Set into the wall is the London Stone. References to this block of limestone go back to 1100 but some interpretations think that it was possibly a Roman mile marker set outside the Governor's palace and from which distances in Roman Britain were measured. The stone has certainly had a very long history. It was the place where contracts were signed between apprentices and their masters and it seems to have had a symbolic status within the city. A plaque on the stone relates how the rebel Jack Cade in 1450 struck his sword on the stone and claimed to be Lord of the City.

Retrace your steps back into the valley of the Walbrook and turn right. On your left at 12 Walbrook is the entrance to the London Mithraeum.

Stop 6

The Temple of Mithras is a relatively recent addition to London's Roman heritage. It was first discovered in 1954 during rebuilding work and became a sensation of post war London with enthusiastic Londoners queuing to see it. It was relocated to Queen Victoria Street for 50 years where it languished by the side of a busy road but has now returned to its original site, seven metres below the new Bloomberg building.

The cult of Mithras flourished in the second and third centuries especially amongst Roman soldiers and temples have been found all over the Roman empire from Northumberland to Israel. There are still many mysteries surrounding the religion but it seems to have its roots in ancient Persian mythologies. Many of the temples were built in caves, often by water and it seems to have been very male dominated. The central symbol is the slaying of a bull by Mithras possibly signifying bravery and sacrifice and the rites seemed to have involved communal meals.

You enter the Mithraeum through a gallery which hosts changing exhibitions. On the ground floor, there is a spectacular display of some of the many artefacts which were found on site. These were wonderfully preserved as the water-logged ground meant even organic materials did not rot. Look, in particular, for the tiny amulet in the shape of a gladiator's mask. After examining the finds you descend towards the Temple  with walls documenting 2,000 years of London's history. There is then an exhibition explaining what is known about Mithraism and you then finally enter the reconstructed temple. There is a short performance where, through the innovative use of sound and light, there is an attempt to recreate the atmosphere of a service.

Leaving the Mithraeum, continue walking up Walbrook. From this valley, archaeologists have unearthed dozens of decapitated skulls which many believe date back to the Boudiccan revolt. Opposite there is a wonderful Christopher Wren church, St. Stephen's Walbrook, which looks relatively modest from the outside but opens up into a spectacular interior.

You reach Bucklersbury. It was at this spot that the main Roman road running east to west bridged the Walbrook. Cross Queen Victoria Street and go through the passage into Poultry. Its strange name has a simple explanation; this was the main market for geese and ducks in medieval times as the carvings on the building opposite remind us. Cross Poultry, bear left and turn right into Old Jewry. This was the centre of the original Jewish community in London prior to their expulsion in 1290. Half way along the street, there is a plaque marking the site of the Great Synagogue. Turn left down the little alley of St Olaf's Place which runs past an old Wren church and right into Ironmonger Lane so called after the ironmongers who used to be based here. They were expelled to the river banks, perhaps one of the first recorded cases of noisy neighbour syndrome. In the basement of No. 11, there is a Roman mosaic, unfortunately it is closed to the public. Turn left down Gresham Street and then right into Guildhall Yard.

Stop 7

In front of you is Guildhall, the City of London's administrative centre. The current building dates back to 1411. However it rests on far older foundations and it was possibly where the inhabitants of Saxon London paid their taxes. For many years archaeologists had puzzled as to the location of London's amphitheatre. They knew there should be one somewhere; after all every great Roman city had one. During routine building works in 1985, archaeologists realised that they had discovered the location of the amphitheatre underneath Guildhall Yard. Its site is marked by the black curved line running round the square. To view the remains enter the art gallery on your left and descend to the basement where there is an atmospheric recreation of the amphi-theatre. At its peak it could seat 6,000 Londoners who came to enjoy gladiator fights, duels with animals and the execution of prisoners.

Leaving the art gallery walk straight across the square and turn right into Aldermanbury and then left into Love Lane, named after the brothels of the medieval period. At the end of Love Lane note the extraordinary tower of St. Alban, Wood Street. Rebuilt by Wren after the Great Fire, the Blitz took away the church but left the tower in splendid isolation. It is now one of the more unusual private houses in London. Carry on through the passageway opposite and you eventually reach Noble Street with a walkway allowing you to inspect more Roman wall. This part of the wall enclosed the fort which housed London's Roman garrison. To see the best preserved part turn right along Noble Street.

Stop 8

You are standing at the south west corner of the ancient Roman fort which defended London against attack from the north and allowed the legions to make a quick foray against external threats. The remains of the walls here have Roman foundations which are still visible. In partic-ular you can see the base of a Roman tower. However, most of what you can see is medieval or later and much of the Roman building is either beneath ground level or has been destroyed over the centuries.

As you walk up Noble Street there are a series of informative panels describing the scene in front of you.

At the end of Noble Street, you reach the aptly named London Wall. To your left is the entrance to the Museum of London with a wonderful display of Roman artefacts all found in London. This would mark an appropriate end to the walk if you can't get enough of all things Roman.

However, if you want to explore one more hidden corner of London, cross the street and walk down opposite towards a car park and find the green space just beyond. Here, you'll find a number of well-preserved medieval towers, built probably in the thirteenth century on Roman foundations. It is a peaceful and secluded spot to end the walk.

Finally

- Nearest stations are St. Paul's, Barbican or Moorgate.
- Nearest pubs are the Lord Raglan in St Martin Le Grand or Slug and Lettuce, Love Lane while the Museum of London has a good cafe.
- For more Roman London, the only place to go is the Museum of London's galleries.

Medieval London

After the Romans left around 410AD, the City of London seems to have been uninhabited for around 400 years; its great walls gradually crumbling. Anglo-Saxon communities resettled the area around what is now Covent Garden in the early seventh century. They also built a church on Tower Hill in 675, the oldest church in the City. The reoccupation of London began in the 880s as Alfred moved inside the walls for protection against Viking attacks leaving behind very little tangible evidence of habitation but two names; Ald Wych (the old town) and the Strand, Saxon for beach. Little of pre-Norman London now remains, but the decision of the last Saxon king, Edward the Confessor, to build both his Palace and Cathedral at Westminster was momentous as it led to the creation of an alternative centre of power to the City.

The Medieval period, which we can define as being from 1066 to 1500, was to see London emerge as one of the great European cities. Over four hundred years its population increased from perhaps 12,000 to around 100,000. Churches, monasteries and cathedrals were built alongside great halls and mansions. Most spectacularly, London was defended in the east by William's great Tower and in the west by Baynard's Castle, the latter long since gone. At Westminster, Edward's Abbey was rebuilt along with Westminster Hall. To the south, the great church of St Mary Overy (now Southwark Cathedral) welcomed visitors to London.

London's wealth was based on trade and especially the trade in wool. From the end of the thirteenth century, London's trade with the continent boomed soon eclipsing all other British ports. The great merchants prospered as they formed themselves into Guilds which controlled and protected their industries. This group of powerful merchants dominated the City's life and, through the Mayor and Aldermen, administered justice, organised military and civic service and collected taxes. Dick Whittington, the most famous mayor, was also famed for his philanthropy. One of his greatest gifts to Londoners was a massive communal toilet, jutting out over the Thames, and seating 64 men and women.

London remained a very cosmopolitan city throughout the Middle Ages as much commerce was in the hands of foreign traders. Jewish bankers, until their expulsion by Edward I in 1290, were concentrated close to the Guildhall in an area still known as Old Jewry. They were replaced by rich Italian merchants who congregated in Lombard Street (after Lombardy). On the Thames, the Hanseatic League, a group of Baltic traders, set up their headquarters in the Steelyard, now covered by Cannon Street Station. Much of the wool trade was in the hands of the Flemish with whom English merchants both competed and collaborated.

From the very beginning, foreigners formed a highly visible minority who were easy scapegoats to blame for any misfortune. A monk writing in the twelfth century could advise: 'If you come to London, pass through it quickly, for I do not at all like that city. All sorts of men crowd together there from every country under the heavens. Each race brings its own vices and its own customs to the city. No-one lives in it without falling into some sort of crime.' (Richard of Devizes).

Much of the wealth flowing through the City ended in the hands of the king, merchants and the church. The church was a massive landlord, owning around a third of the land in London. There were 126 parish churches and nearly thirty monasteries in or close to the City. Their names have come down to us through the centuries; Black-friars, Greyfriars, Whitefriars, Crutched Friars and Austin Friars have all given their names to streets or areas in London. Some did very valuable work such as the monks and nuns of St Mary of Bethlehem who administered the asylum of Bedlam or the brothers of St. Bartholomew's who ran London's oldest and largest hospital. Others were much more of a drain as they demanded tithes from their parishioners.

For ordinary Londoners, life could be short and harsh. Living conditions in the City were cramped and filthy and disease and fire were constant hazards. In 1348, the Black Death arrived killing perhaps forty per cent of London's population. Great burial pits had to be dug as the plague swept through the over-crowded tenements. This catastrophe led to the greatest upheaval in medieval England. As labour became scarcer so the constraints of feudalism in the countryside became more onerous. The royal demands for money to prosecute the 100 years' war and especially the introduction of a poll tax led to the Great Rising or the Peasants' Revolt of 1381. Their demands were radical: 'Things cannot go on well in England nor ever will until everything shall be in common, when there shall be neither vassal nor lord, and all distinctions levelled.'

Tens of thousands of rural workers from Essex and Kent led by Wat Tyler, John Ball and Jack Straw converged on London demanding radical change. They paid homage to their boy king Richard II but demanded he rid himself of his advisors. Let into the City by sympathetic Londoners the rebels attacked and burnt the mansions of the great lords, the monasteries and the offices of lawyers. The gaols were flung open and prisoners released. Royal officials, priors, lawyers and tax collectors were attacked and killed as were any foreigners unfortunate enough to be caught. Among the victims were the Archbishop of Canterbury, the Chancellor of the Exchequer and dozens of Flemings. After three days when London was in the hands of the rebels, the King called them to negotiations at Smithfield. As Wat Tyler talked to the King an argument broke out and the Lord Mayor of London, William Walworth, stabbed Tyler. Grievously wounded, he was taken to St Bartholomew's hospital but was tracked down by the Mayor and beheaded. The nobles' retribution was bloody and long-lasting as they pursued the Rising's participants across eastern England. Although it was defeated, the Peasants' Revolt was a sign that the medieval structures of society were beginning to break down and that social and intellectual change was on the way.

Medieval London has almost entirely disappeared. Henry VIII demolished many of the monasteries and the Great Fire burnt three quarters of the City, destroying 87 churches. Urban improvements and the Blitz took away much of what remained. Despite this some hidden jewels remain and they can still give us an impression of what London could have looked like and how our forebears lived seven hundred years ago.

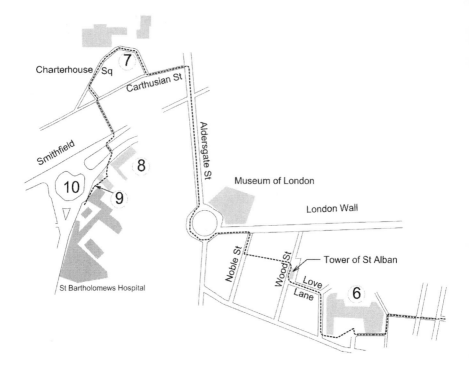

1. Tower Hill Underground

2. St Olave's Church

3. St Andrew Undercroft

4. St Helen's Bishopsgate

5. St Ethelburga's

6. Guildhall

7. Charterhouse Square

8. St Bartholomew The Great

9. Peasants Revolt memorial

10. Smithfield

Details of what you'll see on this walk start on the page following this map...

A walk through Medieval London

This walk skirts round the north and north eastern edge of the city, the only part to escape the Great Fire, taking in some of the precious reminders of medieval London. Further damage to the medieval heritage was caused by the arrival of the railways, the Blitz and the enthusiastic development of the city both by the Victorians and the architects of the last fifty years. There's not much left but we will make the most of it.

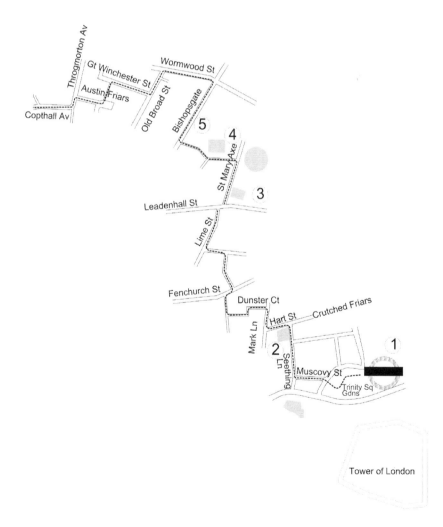

Stop 1

From Tower Hill Underground walk in to Trinity Square. Towards your left you see the greatest medieval building in London, the Tower started by William the Conqueror and added to by a string of medieval monarchs.

Walk in the direction of All Hallows church in the south western corner of Trinity Square. Ten metres before you exit the square you will see to your right a small space surrounded by a low wall. This is the site of the Tower Hill scaffold. This was where in 1381 the rebels of the Peasants Revolt brought the Archbishop of Canterbury, Simon Sudbury, and the Lord High Treasurer, Robert Hales, from the Tower and executed them both. A plaque commemorates them and the many others who died here over the next four hundred years.

Walk down Muscovy Street, past the side of the enormous Port of London Authority building, now a luxury hotel and turn right into Seething Lane. On your left you soon see the macabre entrance to St Olave's Church.

Stop 2

St Olave's is one of London's more famous churches. Its entrance was described by Charles Dickens who called it St Ghastly Grim and it is the church of Samuel Pepys who is buried here along with his wife, Elizabeth. We are visiting it, however, because it is one of the best preserved medieval churches in London. Built originally in the eleventh century to honour a Norwegian saint, the current building dates back to 1450. It has been heavily restored after being damaged in the Blitz but still gives an impression of sanctity and peace. In the left hand corner as you come in there is a stairway guarded by a small gate which leads down to a remarkable slice of London's history. You walk down to a tiny crypt and next to the altar can be seen a covered well. This is said to be where St. Olave rallied his troops alongside his Anglo-Saxon ally, Ethelred the Unready, to drive out Danish invaders. It was during this battle that the defenders pulled down London Bridge to prevent the city being attacked from the south leading to speculation that this incident inspired the nursery rhyme 'London Bridge is falling down'. St Olave's is a typical medieval parish church, just one of the 120 that once were within the city walls. It is small and beautifully decorated and while the decorations date from after the Reformation of the early sixteenth century it gives a good impression of how a medieval church looked.

Walk out of the church through the door opposite into Hart Street. On your right the road becomes Crutched Friars, the site of a monastery founded in 1249 by an order whose monks habitually carried staffs topped with a crucifix, giving them their name. Turn left down Hart Street and then right into Mark Lane. Within a few metres you pass the tower of All Hallows Staining which dates back to the early fourteenth century. Its proximity to St Olave's demonstrates just how numerous these tiny parish churches were in medieval London.

Walk through Dunster Court and cross Fenchurch Street. Heading north, walk through the spectacular architecture of 120 Fenchurch Street. Turn left towards the Lloyds building and then right down Lime Street. At the corner of Leadenhall Street you see one of the most iconic views of London, an ancient church underneath a thoroughly modern building.

Stop 3

This is the church of St Andrew Undershaft, on St Mary Axe, framed by the Gherkin. The church, which is not normally open to the public, is most noteworthy for the memorial to John Stowe, chronicler of Tudor London. The name Undershaft derives from the fact that the great medieval maypole of London used to be erected each year in front of the church until destroyed by rioting apprentices in 1517. Look around and you can see the maypole still commemorated in some of the street architecture. The street's name is also medieval. It reminds us that there was a second church close by called, remarkably, 'St Mary, St Ursula and her 11,000 Virgins'. The church claimed to possess one of the original axes that had beheaded Ursula along with her 11,000 handmaidens in Germany as they returned from a pilgrimage to Rome.

Cross Leadenhall Street and walk through the square to the left of St Mary Axe. In front of you is the church of St Helen's Bishopsgate, one of the most magnificent of the City's medieval churches.

Stop 4

Standing in front of St Helen's, it's immediately clear that there are in fact two churches knocked into one. On the right hand, southern, side is the original parish church dating back to the twelfth century while the left hand side is a nunnery church added in the early thirteenth century. Originally a screen divided the two churches although this did not always prevent a certain amount of fraternisation: in 1385 the nuns were reprimanded for kissing secular persons. While the building survived both the Great Fire and the Blitz it was heavily damaged by two IRA bombs in the 1990s. It was sympathetically restored and today is perhaps the most beautiful and richly ornamented of the City churches. It offers a striking contrast between the wealth and power of the monasteries and the humbler parish churches visited earlier. St Helen's is often used for meetings and lectures and may be locked at other times. If the doors are locked, you can call at the office to the side of the church where the staff will let you enter if possible.

Walk away from the church, down Great St Helen's to Bishopsgate, turn right and in 100 metres you reach the tiny church of St Ethelburga's. Its size and simplicity stand in very marked contrast to the glory of St. Helen's.

Stop 5

St Ethelburga's was very badly damaged by the IRA Bishopsgate bomb and is now a centre for reconciliation and peace. There is a beautiful but tiny garden, a welcome haven from the bustle and noise of Bishopsgate with, somewhat unexpectedly, a circular yurt for meetings. The church itself is very small and was first recorded in 1250 but rebuilt in the early fifteenth century. It is normally open although it often hosts meetings and conferences when access may be restricted.

Continue to walk up Bishopsgate then cross the road at the lights into Wormwood Street. Turn left into Old Broad Street, right into Great Winchester Street and then left down Austin Friars Passage. You are now in the heart of the old Augustinian Friary, one of the greatest monasteries in London from around 1260 to its dissolution almost 300 years later. Thomas Cromwell, who led on the dissolution of the monasteries, owned property here until Henry VIII had him arrested and executed. The Dutch Church stands on the site of the old friary church. It was first granted to 'Germans and other strangers' by Edward VI in 1550. It is the oldest Dutch Protestant church in the world but was completely destroyed in the Blitz and had to be rebuilt in the 1950s.

Walk along Austin Friars into Throgmorton Avenue, turn left then right into Copthall Avenue and then straight on through the tiny alleys (Telegraph Street, Great Bell Alley and Mason's Avenue) which still bear witness to the medieval street plan. You finally arrive at the entrance to Guildhall Yard.

Stop 6

Guildhall's history goes back to at least the twelfth century with the current building dating back to 1440. It may well stand on an Anglo-Saxon Guildhall where citizens paid their taxes. That in turn was sited on top of the Roman Amphitheatre which we visited in an earlier walk.

Today the complex houses the City of London Corporation which is the Governing Body for the historic centre of London. Its structure, based on the Lord Mayor, the Court of Aldermen, Freemen and Livery Companies of the City, has evolved from the time of the Norman Conquest. Guildhall itself is used for great ceremonial occasions and is often closed to the public. If it is open the entrance is at the side opposite to the Art Gallery (which itself is one of the best unknown galleries of London). If you can get in, you will be treated to one of the great medieval halls of Britain.

Leave Guildhall by walking north up Aldermanbury past the excellent Guildhall library and the tiny police museum; turn left into Love Lane to stand in front of St Alban's Tower one of the strangest houses in London. St Alban's was founded possibly 1200 years ago, destroyed in the fire, rebuilt by Wren then destroyed in the Blitz leaving only its tower behind. Today it is a private house marooned on its own traffic island.

Walk through the passage in front of you and then turn right along Noble Street, left along London Wall. At the roundabout turn right to walk along Aldersgate Street until you reach Carthusian Street; here turn left and walk into Charterhouse Square. (Those of you who know the Barbican well may be able to find a more pleasant route along the walkways but it can be very confusing!)

Stop 7

Charterhouse Square was originally one of the great burial pits of London during the Black Death of 1348. Tens of thousands of bodies were interred here. A great Carthusian monastery was then built on the site. It became the first monastery to be suppressed by Henry VIII and the prior and monks paid a bloody price for their resistance with the prior being hung, drawn and quartered and the monks being starved to death. After that episode resistance to the dissolution of the monasteries declined, unsurprisingly. The site then became a great stately home owned by the richest commoner in London, Thomas Sutton. For the last four hundred years it has been an almshouse and a school although the school moved out to Surrey in the nineteenth century. Inside the complex there is a free museum which takes you into the chapel. While much of the buildings date from 1611 or later, the complex and especially the museum gives you an idea of the scale and wealth of the monastery before its dissolution. It is a fascinating place and if you want to find out more, the tours of Charterhouse are highly recommended.

Leave the Charterhouse by walking down Charterhouse Street and along Lindsey Street at the east end of the Smithfield meat market complex. Turn right along Long Lane and then immediately left into Rising Sun Court. There is a wonderful view in front of you; the black and white church of St Bartholomew the Great, framed in a medieval alleyway. Walk into the church yard on your right.

Stop 8

The church charges admission but it is well worth paying. St Bartholomew's was founded in 1123 by Rahere, supposedly a court jester to Henry I as the priory church of a great Augustinian monastery.

The original church escaped both the great fire and the Blitz which took so many of the medieval buildings of London. The present building, however, is only a fraction of the great medieval church as the majority of it was destroyed during the dissolution of the monasteries. What remains is very beautiful and it has been used as a set in numerous films including Four Weddings and a Funeral, Shakespeare in Love and Robin Hood: Prince of Thieves.

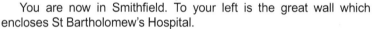

Leave the church through the atmospheric Tudor gatehouse built on a thirteenth century arch.

You are now in Smithfield. To your left is the great wall which encloses St Bartholomew's Hospital.

Stop 9

Just by the corner, you will see a monument on the wall to the Peasants Revolt of 1381. The memorial, unveiled by film maker Ken Loach, bears witness to where Wat Tyler rode out to negotiate with the king and where he was killed by William Walworth, Lord Mayor of London.

Stop 10

Smithfield has had a bloody history over the years as a place of execution. We walk past a memorial to the Protestant Martyrs of the 1550s which we will visit on a future walk to arrive at our final stop. It is often marked by Scottish flags because this commemorates where Sir William Wallace, Hollywood's Braveheart, was executed by Edward I. This clash between Scotland and England was one of the great conflicts of medieval Britain. Wallace's death did little to stop the conflict; within ten years Robert the Bruce won a stunning victory at Bannockburn guaranteeing Scottish independence for the next 300 years.

Finally

Smithfield has some great pubs and restaurants. The nearest stations are Thameslink, St Paul's or Farringdon.

Reformation London

By 1500, London was one of the great European cities. Its population was growing rapidly as it reached 100,000 probably for the first time in its history. It was growing richer as the wool trade, in particular, expanded. Above all the end of the Wars of the Roses finally led to peace and stability in the realm. The accession of Henry VIII in 1509 seemed to promise the arrival of a new era for England and London as this cultured, renaissance prince came to the throne. However, these hopes were soon dashed. Within a quarter of a century, England was racked by a bitter religious feud between Catholic and Protestant which was to dominate politics for the next two hundred years.

In 1509 England, London and the monarchy were all staunchly Catholic. It was true that there had been an underground English tradition of opposition to some of the core tenets of Catholicism notably the Lollard 'heresy'. That tradition had been founded by John Wycliffe who first translated the bible into English in the 1380s and whose attacks on the church in Rome helped lay the basis for the Reformation 150 years later. That started in Germany where in 1517 Martin Luther publicly challenged some of the practices and beliefs of Catholicism, in particular its perceived perversion of bible teaching and its monetary corruption. To begin with Henry remained loyally Catholic, indeed the Pope named him as Defender of the Faith, a title which English monarchs continue to use to this day. He and his close friend Sir Thomas More continued to persecute and burn Protestant dissidents. But all this was about to change.

The story of the Reformation in Britain is often told along the lines of Henry VIII having the hots for Anne Boleyn and, indeed, any other pretty girl at court. Of course, that may have been partly true but the reality was much more complex. At its heart was the urgent need for a male heir to consolidate the Tudor dynasty. After all Henry's father had come to power through civil war and there was no recent precedent for a woman taking the throne in such a troubled time. Henry's wife, Catherine of Aragon, had a daughter Mary but a son was urgently needed and Catherine, six years older than Henry, showed no signs of producing a boy. To get a divorce in order to take another, more fertile wife, Henry needed the permission of the Pope. That wasn't forthcoming partly because the Pope was in thrall to Catherine's nephew, the Spanish Emperor Charles V. As a result, Henry, in order to get a new wife, had to break from the Pope and set himself up as head of a newly formed Church of England so that he could determine church law regarding his divorce. Those who could not accept this change such as Sir Thomas More and John Fisher died at Tower Hill. Liturgically, however, relatively little changed and Henry continued to burn Catholic resisters and Protestant 'heretics' alike.

Socially, however, the economic and political power of the church was destroyed. In particular, the great monasteries which so dominated London life were dissolved and their property seized by the King. First to go was the great Carthusian monastery near Smithfield whose Prior, John Houghton, resisted and was hung, drawn and quartered for his obduracy. Of his fellow monks, nine starved to death in Newgate Prison and the last was executed on Tower Hill. The rest of the London monasteries took note and resistance ended. The monasteries were sold off and most were destroyed although some of their work was preserved notably at St Bartholomew's whose hospital still survives. The dissolution provided an enormous financial windfall for Henry. Much went to fund his and his favourites' lavish life style but still more went to fund the new English Navy.

However religious conflict was not ended. The two hundred years after Henry's death were dominated by the struggles over religion.

The short reign of Edward VI led to a decisive break with the Catholic religion. Many London churches were stripped of their decorations and treasures as the new Protestantism banned the veneration of images and rewrote the liturgy. By 1550 only one London church even retained an altar.

The Protestant tide was firmly reversed with the death of Edward and the accession of Mary to the throne. The daughter of Catherine of Aragon she was firmly Catholic and was soon married to the King of Spain, the dominant Catholic power. She repealed her father's religious laws and leading Protestants were imprisoned. In her short reign 280 protestants were burned including the bishops Cranmer, Latimer and Ridley earning her the nickname Bloody Mary. On her death, her half-sister, Elizabeth, daughter of Anne Boleyn, finally brought some resolution to the religious turmoil. She pursued a more moderate Protestantism becoming the Supreme Governor of the Church of England. The new church retained some elements of Catholicism such as the wearing of vestments and repealed the heresy laws. Elizabeth rejected making 'windows into men's souls' and the hunt for heresy was stilled. While some, especially Catholic priests, continued to die for their faith, after twenty years of tumult, chaos and repression, England was at relative peace.

The Catholic Protestant conflict, however, was not yet over and it continued to divide Britain in the following centuries. The Gunpowder Plot 1605, the Civil War 1642, the Glorious Revolution 1688 and the Jacobin uprisings of 1715 and 1745 all had their roots, at least in part, in the clash of faiths.

London had been at the epicentre of this great conflict between Catholicism and Protestantism and four hundred years on it is still possible to trace where these momentous events occurred.

On this walk we start from St. Paul's, the centre of religious life in the City of London, and end in Clerkenwell, The Clerks' (i.e. Priests') Well, the centre of one of the biggest monasteries in London. Along the way we will come across religious adherents fighting and dying for their faith as well as a much later bunch of radical atheists.

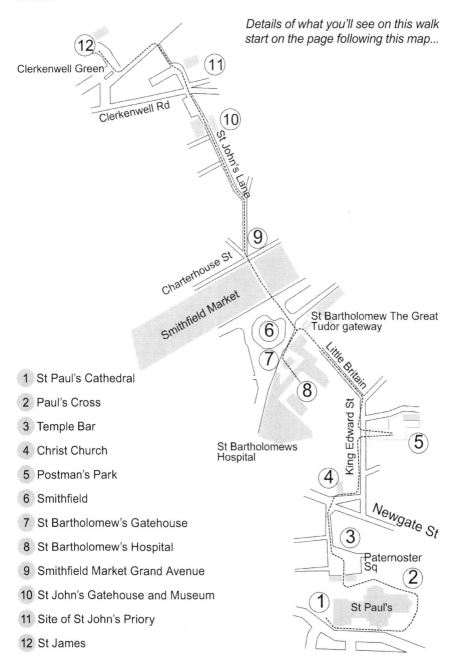

Details of what you'll see on this walk start on the page following this map...

1 St Paul's Cathedral

2 Paul's Cross

3 Temple Bar

4 Christ Church

5 Postman's Park

6 Smithfield

7 St Bartholomew's Gatehouse

8 St Bartholomew's Hospital

9 Smithfield Market Grand Avenue

10 St John's Gatehouse and Museum

11 Site of St John's Priory

12 St James

A walk through Reformation London

Stop 1

We start on the steps of the Cathedral, Christopher Wren's greatest church and the symbol of Protestant power in London. Its massive exterior looks down Ludgate Hill dominating the view from Fleet Street. Most Londoners assume the statue by the steps is that of Queen Victoria but they're mistaken. In fact, it is another of our small, plump queens. It is Queen Anne who was reigning when the cathedral was completed and who can be seen perhaps as the first Protestant monarch truly secure on the throne. Queen Anne by the way was very small and very plump. She was only around 4 foot 10 but weighed an impressive 350 pounds.

Walk round the south side of the cathedral and enter the gardens at the back and look for the golden statue on top of a high plinth.

Stop 2

This commemorates Paul's Cross where for 200 years the debates over scripture and liturgy were conducted and Londoners listened to and sometimes disagreed with government pronouncements of orthodoxy. Most famously, Bishop Bourne at the start of Mary's reign almost provoked a riot and had a dagger thrown at him as he preached the Catholic faith. In the following century it was where the competing brands of Protestantism fought to gain adherents. Lectures were given here including one by John Donne, the great metaphysical poet of the 1600s. The actual position of the cross is marked on the ground 20 metres south east of the monument.

Carry on round the north side of the cathedral until you see on your right the entrance to Paternoster Square through the great triumphal arch of Temple Bar.

Stop 3

This monument, designed by Christopher Wren, used to stand at the entrance to the City where Fleet Street becomes the Strand. It marked the spot where the monarch had to stop and ask permission of the Lord Mayor to enter the City. Like many monuments of the time it had a very political purpose. On the south side of the gate are sculptures of Charles I and Charles II while on the north side it is James I and his queen, Anne of Denmark. With

the arch, Charles II is validating the legitimacy of the House of Stuart pointing out that there are three generations of monarchs overseeing London despite one having lost his head.

The Bar was removed in the 1870s and ended up as the great entrance to the stately home in Hertfordshire of the brewer Henry Meux It was rebuilt in its current position in 2004.

Walk through the Bar into Paternoster Square and past another magnificent column with a golden urn on top. It has, unfortunately, absolutely no historical significance; rather it is a ventilation shaft for the Central Line! Rather more pleasing is another statue in the Square by Elizabeth Frink, called the Paternoster.

Walk straight through the Square until you reach Newgate Street and in front of you are the ruins of Christ Church.

Cross the street and enter the gardens of the church.

Stop 4

Christ Church was one of the great Christian centres of London. Originally, it was the church of the Franciscan monastery, the Grey Friars and was the second biggest church in the City. It demonstrates just how powerful and rich the medieval church was with the great cathedral of St. Paul's just next door. It was also a place of royal burial with four queens; Marguerite, Joan, Isabella and Eleanor being interred here. In Eleanor's case, it was just her heart with the rest of her being buried at Amesbury.

The Priory was dissolved by Henry VIII and became a parish church. Destroyed in the Fire, it was rebuilt by Wren but only to a third of its previous size. Badly damaged in the Blitz only the tower and some of the retaining walls were preserved. The garden traces the shape of Wren's design and remains a peaceful place in summer.

Walk up King Edward Street noting Queen Isabella Way on your left and the statue to Rowland Hill, creator of the modern postal service. It stands outside the General Post Office once the hub of London's communication system. Cross the street and enter the old churchyard.

Stop 5

This is Postman's Park, home to one of the most extraordinary memorials in London. Partly in reaction to Victoria's Golden Jubilee, the artist G. F. Watts created 'The Memorial to Heroic Self Sacrifice', where ordinary people who died saving others could be commemorated. He and his wife built a loggia where tiles commemorate those heroes from the past. Most tiles date back to the Victorian era but new ones are beginning to be added once more. (Apologies - this has little if anything to do with the religious battles of 500 years ago, but every Londoner needs to know and visit this wonderful little corner of Victorian London.) But the park does have a link with the religious debates of the post-Reformation. At no. 5 Little Britain, overlooking the park, John and Charles Wesley were said to have had their evangelical conversion leading to the foundation of Methodism in 1738.

Retrace your steps and turn right, walking down Little Britain eventually reaching Smithfield.

Stop 6

Smithfield is one of the most historic sites of London. The original name was Smooth Field and it lay just outside the city walls and overlooking the valley of the Fleet, a convenient place for everything the City didn't want. For a thousand years it was the abattoir for London as Cowcross Street reminds us. Dickens wrote of crossing the market ankle deep in gore. It was partly due to his efforts that Smithfield became a meat market with the slaughtering taking place in Islington. But it wasn't just animals that were killed here, Smithfield was one of the main places of execution of religious dissenters during the turmoil of the Reformation.

Between the memorial to William Wallace and to the Peasants' Revolt, there is a third plaque to the Protestant Martyrs who died in the reign of Mary I. Six are commemorated but hundreds more, both Catholics and Protestants, died here. The first recorded execution for heresy here was of a Lollard in 1401 and the last, another radical Protestant, in 1612.

Look to your left, to the entrance of St Bartholomew the Great with its Tudor gatehouse. It is claimed that Mary I used the second story window to look out on the burning martyrs below whilst eating her favourite meal of lamb chops. The story is almost certainly untrue but just reminds us that history is written by the victors, in this case to vilify their opponents. What is true is that the arch was owned by one of the great villains of English History, Richard Rich. Amongst many other crimes, he committed perjury against Thomas More to have him condemned as a traitor and  personally tortured Protestants. He served Henry VIII, Edward, Mary and Elizabeth, enriching himself under each monarch and persecuted Catholic and Protestant alike according to the changes in state policy.

Walk away from the gate house towards the entrance to St Bartholomew's Hospital, noting the damage to the walls. This was caused by air raids both in the Blitz and in the rarely remembered Zeppelin raids of the First World War.

Stop 7

Stand outside the gatehouse, looking into the hospital grounds. St. Bartholomew's Hospital is the oldest hospital in Britain and has operated from this site for 900 years. It was founded in 1123 by Rahere a favourite courtier to Henry I and who is buried in the nearby church of St. Bartholomew's the Great. Its Augustinian monastery was dissolved by Henry VIII but St Bartholomew's was allowed to continue as London's major hospital. Above you in the gatehouse you'll see a statue to Henry VIII in London. It was erected years later to commemorate Henry's 'benevolence' in not destroying the monastery.

Walk through the gateway into the hospital. On your left is the church of St. Bartholomew the Less, the hospital's chapel. The church has been on the site since the end of the twelfth century although the oldest part of the current building is the tower which dates from the fifteenth. The interior is late eighteenth century and it remains a peaceful and evocative place. It is certainly worth a visit.

Stop 8

Walk further into the Hospital and on your left is a small but interesting museum outlining the history of the Hospital and aspects of medical science and health care since the middle ages. Its true glory though is concealed through a door half way round the museum behind which is the entrance to the Great Hall. William Hogarth painted two enormous murals depicting biblical scenes with a medical interest; the Pool of Bethesda and the Good Samaritan. The story goes that Hogarth, who was born round the corner in Bartholomew's Close, painted these pictures for free to demonstrate the power of English painting as he was outraged that the original commission had gone to an Italian painter. Look carefully at the picture of the Pool in front of you and you may see that the bystanders come with a wide range of medical conditions including tuberculosis, gonorrhoea and liver cancer.

Retrace your steps back to Smithfield and go through the Grand Avenue which bisects the market.

Stop 9

Along the way, there are informative panels that detail the history of Smithfield and the many nefarious activities that have taken place there. Over the years it has served as an abattoir, a jousting ground and hosted an annual fair where 'wife-selling' took place well into the nineteenth century. Today it remains the largest fresh meat market in Britain.

At the end of the Grand Avenue if you've not visited Charterhouse on the previous walk looking at Medieval London, you could take the opportunity now. It's well worth visiting as it's only a few hundred metres to your right. The museum gives a good impression of a London religious house as well as being the site of the first monastery to be dissolved.

Otherwise cross Charterhouse Street and go down St. John Street and then bear left down St John's Lane.

Look out for a plaque commemorating a Zeppelin attack during the First World War. You'll also pass an unappealing alley way called Passing Alley. Its original name was slightly different; for 250 years the 'a' used to be an 'i'!

Stop 10

In front of you stands a Tudor gatehouse which led to the great monastery of St. John. This was founded in the twelfth century and was the home of the Knights Hospitaller who had responsibility for the medical care of crusaders and pilgrims. The Gatehouse was re-built in 1504 and the monastery was dissolved in 1538. After Dissolution, the main buildings of the monastery were sold off and much was destroyed. Some of its stone was used to build the Duke of Somerset's enormous palace on the banks of the Thames. The Gatehouse was  preserved after the dissolution and had an illustrious and varied history. Shakespeare came here to present his plays for approval to the Lord Chamberlain, the official censor. Dr Johnson was employed here as a journalist on 'The Gentleman's Magazine'. It was also the childhood home of the painter, William Hogarth. Today, it houses a beautiful small museum detailing the history of the Order of St. John's. It's well worth a visit as is a more detailed tour of the whole complex. One exhibit in the museum is a painting bought as a Caravaggio. When the provenance was disputed an expensive legal battle ensued before deciding against the buyer.

After visiting the museum cross Clerkenwell Road into St John's Square.

Stop 11

In the square in front of you, a circle is picked out in dark bricks. This is the perimeter of the priory church of St John's. It is circular as it is based on the Church of the Holy Sepulchre in Jerusalem, built on the site of the tomb of Christ. Inside the church's grounds there is a beautiful garden as well as a crypt. This houses exhibits linked to the main museum in the Gatehouse. It can be visited as part of the official tours of St. John's.

Walk on through Jerusalem Passage and you emerge into Clerkenwell Green on your left.

The Green has not seen grass for many years but the Well that watered the clerks can still be seen on Farringdon Lane in the north west corner of the square. The Green also marks the boundary between the St. John's monastery to the south and the nunnery of St. Mary's to the north and it was here that mystery plays were performed in early medieval London.

The Green later became the centre of radical London for over a hundred years. The Marx Memorial Library is housed on the north side of the Green. Marx never studied there but it was the headquarters of the first British political party to be inspired by Marx; the Social Democratic Federation. Later both Lenin and Stalin were based there in Czarist exile. You can still visit Lenin's study where he edited the revolutionary paper Iskra at the beginning of the twentieth century.

However, it is the church in front of us that is our final destination.

Stop 12

St James' stands on the site of the nunnery church but was rebuilt in 1792 in classical style. Its interior is beautiful and retains some memorials from the much older church. More modern is a memorial to the victims of the 'Fenian Conspiracy', a plot to rescue Irish nationalists from nearby Clerkenwell Prison which killed 12 innocent bystanders. Most importantly for this walk, there is a memorial to the 66 Protestant Martyrs burnt by Queen Mary at Smithfield in her vain attempt to turn back the Reformation.

It is a poignant reminder of the human cost of this turbulent period in the religious life of London, not just for those it mentions but for the hundreds it does not. For Protestants also burnt Catholics; indeed Protestants burnt other Protestants all in the name of their true faith.

On such a sobering thought, it's probably time to head into one or other of the excellent eateries that surround Clerkenwell Green. If you're looking for a spot of atheism after all that religion you can always head to the Crown where you can sit in the same room where Lenin and Stalin met for a pint or two after a hard day's agitating.

Finally

The nearest station is Farringdon. There are lots of cafes and restaurants as well as pubs in the area.

A really interesting and beautiful place is St Ethelreda's in Ely Place. It is very old and was used by the Spanish Ambassador as a chapel after the Reformation providing sanctuary for persecuted Catholics.

The Great Fire of London

The Great Fire of London was the greatest catastrophe to hit the City since Boudicca 1600 years before. The 1666 fire destroyed the homes of 70,000 of its 80,000 inhabitants and 87 of its 120 churches. It was a key moment in London's history and led to its rebuilding as a recognisably modern city. While the story of the Great Fire is well known to schoolchildren everywhere, the political and economic context and its consequences are often ignored.

London in 1666 was a deeply divided and often paranoid society. Charles II had only recently been restored to the throne after the bloody Civil War, the execution of his father and the protectorate of Oliver Cromwell. Far from being the 'Merry Monarch' of legend, Charles II was a highly divisive figure. He pursued those responsible for his father's death even to the point of disinterring the body of Oliver Cromwell and ritually beheading it. He was suspected of being a closet Catholic and many members of his family, including his wife and brother, were open devotees of the old faith. But London was a Protestant city and regarded Charles with deep suspicion. Further the country was fighting a bitter naval war against the Dutch and was losing badly. There were constant rumours of foreign invasion. Worst of all London in 1665 had just been hit by the Great Plague which had killed a quarter of its population. Could it get any worse? Perhaps it could; because wasn't the following year the Devil's number: 1 666?

The fire started in Thomas Farriner's baker's shop in Pudding Lane in the heart of the city early in the morning of Sunday 2 September. It followed a long hot summer and the wooden houses that made up much of London's housing were tinder dry. At around 3 am on Sunday morning the diarist Samuel Pepys was woken by his maid. He saw the fire was 300 metres away and the strong easterly wind was tending to push the fire westward, away from his house, so he promptly went back to bed. By Sunday morning, however, the fire was clearly a major problem and Pepys went to see the king to plead for urgent help. The man who was supposed to be leading the fight against the fire, Thomas Bloodworth, Lord Mayor of London, was ineffective and ignored. By the afternoon, the blaze had spread to the river cutting off the water supply and was clearly out of control. Attempts to put out the fire had effectively stopped and Londoners concentrated on saving their possessions and fleeing its approach. The king overrode the City administration and placed his brother, James, Duke of York, in command of firefighting efforts. Much of the latter's initial efforts in the first two days were devoted to rescuing foreigners being attacked by the mob as rumours spread of sabotage.

The fire spread with astonishing speed and ferocity. St. Paul's, which had become the repository of books, documents and valuables, was ablaze partly due to the wooden scaffolding erected by a young architect who was repairing the roof. The architect's name was Christopher Wren. John Evelyn described how, as the Cathedral burned, molten lead ran down the streets in a stream as St Paul's lead roof was consumed. By now temperatures had reached over 1200 degrees Celsius and the fire was so ferocious that it was spreading against the easterly wind, threatening the Tower of London with its stocks of gunpowder. In the west the fire had leapt the River Fleet and the mansions of the wealthy were now at its mercy. There was nothing to stop the fire reaching Westminster.

Only on Wednesday was the fire finally brought under control. James ordered swathes of houses to be blown up or pulled down to create fire breaks. Crucially, the wind began to die down and the fire was gradually quelled. By Thursday morning Pepys ascended the tower of All Hallows and contemplated 'the saddest sight of desolation that I ever saw'.

London was in ruins. Three quarters of the City had been burned, tens of thousands had been left homeless and were camping out in the fields surrounding London. Emotions ran high. All sorts of wild explanations were put forward about the reasons for the fire: it was God's punishment for greed or for licentiousness or for disobedience. It was said to be started by the Catholics, the Protestants, the Dutch or the French. Some even blamed the Duke of York, the future James II and one of the few heroes of the fire, as having started it. Anti-Catholic prejudice, in particular, flourished and the blame for the fire was ascribed to them for the next 150 years. A scapegoat was needed and one was duly found. An innocent French protestant, Robert Hubert, was arrested and executed for starting the fire even though it emerged he hadn't even been in London on the day it started.

The Fire has since generated other myths. Some believed that the Fire wiped out the plague. While it's true that since the Fire London has not been revisited by plague it is surely only a coincidence. After all, only 70% of the City was destroyed and the suburbs which were often the poorest and deadliest places where disease flourished were left untouched.

It was also said that only a very few people died. It's true that only six deaths were reported and these were mainly foreigners attacked by the mob. But this death toll seems difficult to believe. The fire at times spread extremely rapidly and the old and infirm may not have had time to escape. After the fire, John Evelyn talked of the stench of bodies underneath the ruins. Some historians now believe that hundreds, perhaps even a few thousand, died in the fire.

Ambitious plans to rebuild London were presented by Christopher Wren, John Evelyn and others even while the fire still smouldered. But these ambitious plans were never realised. Property rights were sacrosanct and such was the urgency to rehouse the homeless that, in the end, new houses were built on the original medieval street pattern. Wren's contribution was not the new city that he had planned but his 51 churches squeezed into existing plots. The rich, however, took the opportunity to move out of the overcrowded city and with the development of new suburbs in Soho, Holborn and Mayfair began the relentless move westwards, which was to last for the next three centuries.

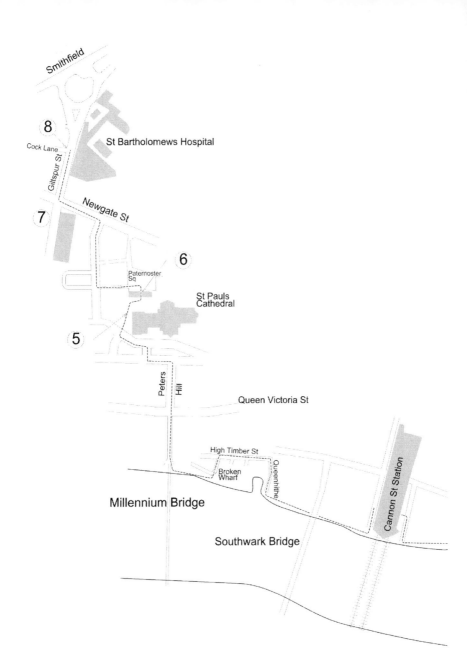

Smithfield

8

Cock Lane

Giltspur St

St Bartholomews Hospital

7

Newgate St

6

Paternoster Sq

St Pauls Cathedral

5

Peters Hill

Queen Victoria St

High Timber St

Broken Wharf

Queenhithe

Millennium Bridge

Southwark Bridge

Cannon St Station

Walking the Great Fire of London

In this walk we follow Samuel Pepys from his home, to the epicentre of the fire and then to where it was finally extinguished in the north west of the city.

1 Tower Hill Station

2 St Olave's Church

3 St Magnus the Martyr

4 The Monument

5 St Paul's Cathedral

6 Temple Bar

7 Old Bailey - site of Newgate Prison

8 Pye Corner

Details of what you'll see on this walk start on the page which follows this map...

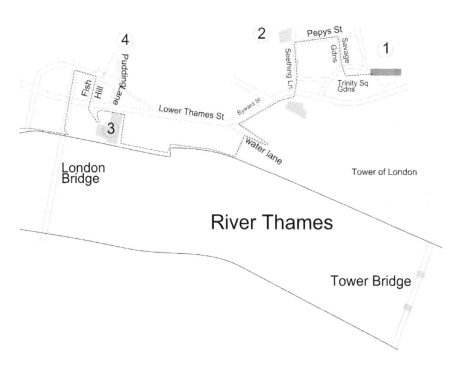

Stop 1

From Tower Hill Station walk into Trinity Square. This is the centre of maritime London and Samuel Pepys knew it well since he was the top civil servant in the Admiralty. On your right is Trinity House responsible for all the inshore waters of Britain including its lighthouses, harbours and navigation. Pepys was elected its master in 1676.

Walk past Trinity House and turn to your right down Savage Gardens past the old Port of London Authority building and turn left into Pepys Street, named because he worked on the left hand side and lived on the right. At the top of the road is St. Olave's Church.

Stop 2

St. Olave's Church is one of London's most beautiful medieval churches. Built around 1450, it survived the Great Fire and has been mentioned by Dickens who called it St. Ghastly Grim due to its somewhat grisly entrance. This is Pepys' church and as you enter the churchyard look to the right and above the main entrance. There is a  plaque marking the spot where Pepys had a private entrance built so that he could enter the church late but unnoticed.

Inside the church, there are memorials to both Pepys and his long-suffering wife, Elisabeth, who seems to be keeping an eye on her restless and randy husband, 300 years after their deaths. There is much to see in the church including a very ancient crypt where legend has it, St Olave rallied Londoners against the invading Danes.

When finished, retrace your steps out of the churchyard and then turn right into Seething Lane. Walk down fifty metres and on your left you'll pass Seething Lane Gardens with a monument to Pepys on the site of the old Admiralty Offices where he was employed.

Carry on past Muscovy Street, cross Byward Street to All Hallows Church. It was from the spire of this church that Pepys saw 'the saddest sight of desolation that I ever saw'. The church was only narrowly saved, the fire scorching its porch. All Hallows marks the eastern most boundary of the fire. It, the Admiralty offices and most importantly the Tower of London with its 600,000 pounds of gunpowder were saved through the efforts of William Penn, father of the founder of Pennsylvania, who blew up a swathe of houses to create a fire break.

Walk down Byward Street and go down the stairs to Water Lane to meet the river. In 1666 the riverbank was lined with warehouses with highly flammable stores full of wood, paper, oil, alcohol and, most worryingly, gunpowder. Once these warehouses caught fire on Sunday afternoon, London was doomed. Those fighting the fire could no longer reach the river to get the water needed to put the fire out, the fire increased in intensity and civil authority collapsed.

Walk along the river and once past the blue glass building, turn right down the passageway and then left on Lower Thames Street.

Stop 3

Walk into the entrance of St. Magnus the Martyr. The church was the first to be destroyed in the fire and one of the first to be rebuilt by Christopher Wren.

The courtyard was the entrance to the old London Bridge and inside the church there is a model of the medieval bridge complete with its wooden houses. It also shows the fire break on the bridge which prevented the flames from reaching Southwark. Despite this, fires did break out on the south bank as sparks flew high up into the air and then landed on Southwark's thatched roofs. Thankfully they were speedily extinguished.

Inside the church there is an even more remarkable exhibit, an original seventeenth century fire engine. One glance at it, with its rudimentary design and limited capacity, would show the enormous difficulties faced by the firefighters of 1666.

Leave the church and cross the road to go up Fish Street Hill.

Stop 4

In 80 metres you are standing in front of the Monument to the Great Fire, designed by Christopher Wren and Robert Hooke. It was completed ten years after the fire and its height marks the same distance to the site of Thomas Farriner's bakery in Pudding Lane. A plaque just to the east of the monument marks the spot where the fire broke out.

Around the sides of the Monument are inscriptions in Latin describing the effects of the Fire. Look carefully at the plaque on the north side. It describes how the fire started, the damage it caused and how it was extinguished. You'll notice that there is a gap in the inscription about three quarters of the way down. The phrase that used to be there until the 1820s were 'but Popish frenzy which wrought such horrors, is not yet quenched'. In other words, the official explanation for 150 years was that the Fire was caused by the Catholics.

Now look at the astonishing sculpture on the west face. This is the official view of the Fire in pictorial form. On the top left, fire is raging and a female figure representing London and holding its ceremonial sword lies prostrate on the ground. To the right Charles II holds the plans for the rebuilding of London in his hand while behind him stands his brother, the future James II. They stand on a hate filled figure, Envy, who is devouring her own heart. Various deities are, at Charles' command, handing London gifts while, at the top right, workers are already rebuilding the city. But this interpretation cut little ice with Londoners. Within days some agitators were blaming James for starting the fire and on his accession to the throne opposition to him grew. His rule was short and he was overthrown in the Glorious Revolution of 1688.

With your back to the carving, walk up Monument Street and turn left onto London Bridge. Go down the stairs on your left to rejoin the river bank and walk along the path under the bridge. As you look southward you will soon see the Anchor pub on the other bank with its distinctive bright red doors and windows. This was where Pepys went on the first day of the fire and reported that: 'we saw the fire as only one entire arch of fire from this to the other side of the bridge and in a bow up the hill for an arch of above a mile long; it made me weep to see it'.

Carry on down the river bank and you will soon pass under Southwark Bridge. In the underpass there are some fine tiles which reproduce London before and after the Great Fire. In particular, there is a great view of old St Paul's before and after fire. It is a vivid demonstration of the destruction caused in 1666.

Continue along the north bank until you come to Queenhithe. This unprepossessing inlet has a remarkable history: it was almost certainly a wharf in Roman times and was the first wharf of Saxon London. It also played a role in the Great Fire as Charles II landed here to review and, indeed, to participate in fire-fighting efforts. You're forced away from the river bank at Queenhithe for a few hundred metres. Walk down High Timber Street and then third left into Broken Wharf to rejoin the riverbank.

Walk up the steps underneath the Millennium Bridge until you emerge on Peter Hill with a wonderful view of St Paul's. Walk towards St Paul's where as you come to St Paul's Churchyard there is, appropriately, a statue to the firefighters of London and the nation. Look up at the wall of St. Paul's in front of you and you should spot an engraving of a phoenix arising from the flames with the motto Resurgam (I shall rise again) written on it.

Walk round to your left to stand on the steps in front of the main entrance to St Paul's.

Stop 5

St Paul's Cathedral was perhaps the greatest casualty of the fire. Many thought that the empty space of the churchyard and the Cathedral's great stone walls would make it impregnable to the ravages of the fire. The booksellers who dominated the area had hurried to save their stocks in the crypt and many wealthier citizens had stored valuables inside the church. However. the fire was relentless. By now, temperatures of 1500 degrees Celsius were being generated. Wooden scaffolding on the tower caught fire and

the diarist John Evelyn described how 'the stones of Paules flew like granados (grenades), the lead melting down the streetes in a streame'. St Paul's was totally gutted and the walls had to be pulled down. The burning of the Cathedral was a disaster yet it also provided an opportunity for Christopher Wren to create his Baroque masterpiece. It took almost forty years to complete and is one of London's great buildings. Look out for the golden pineapples at the top of the towers: they are a symbol of wealth and welcome. In the seventeenth century they were one of the most prized commodities in the world. Keep your eyes open and you will soon be seeing pineapples everywhere.

Walk around the steps and on your left you will see Temple Bar guarding the passage way between the church yard and Paternoster Square.

Stop 6

This imposing gate used to stand at the entrance to the City on Fleet Street. Designed by Christopher Wren and erected in 1672, it carries statues of Charles I and Charles II perhaps to symbolise the continuity of the royal line and the illegitimacy of the regicide.

Walk through the Bar into Paternoster Square, turn first left towards Amen Corner (unfortunately nothing to do with the group led by Andy Fairweather Low!) on Ave Maria Lane. Turn right towards Newgate Street. As you walk, you'll notice a lovely Victorian frieze inspired by the Arts and Crafts movement illustrating the production of cutlery. Turn left onto Newgate Street and soon you'll reach the forbidding walls of the Central Criminal Court, better known as the Old Bailey.

Stop 7

This corner was the site of the infamous Newgate Prison. Over the centuries it had housed thousands of prisoners including Captain Kidd, Daniel Defoe, Oscar Wilde and Sir Thomas Mallory. It, too, burned in

1666. Abandoned by the gaolers as the Fire approached, the prisoners escaped just in time. By now, the Fire was being brought under control. Charles and James were ordering the pulling down of blocks of houses in the north and west of the City and crucially the wind was dying down. The Fire still had the power however to damage, but not destroy, the church of St Sepulchre opposite you. There used to be a passage that led from the church to the prison so that condemned prisoners could be tended to by the clergy and the pub opposite claims that its cellars were once prison cells.

Walk down Giltspur Street noting London's first drinking fountain set into the railings of St Sepulchre; the old watch house built to deter body snatchers at the beginning of the nineteenth century and the plaque to Charles Lamb with its optimistic claim that he was 'Perhaps the most loved name in English literature'. Perhaps indeed. Giltspur Street leads straight to St Bartholomew's Hospital, London's oldest and largest. If that had burnt disaster would have turned to catastrophe.

You arrive at the corner of Cock Lane, named after the medieval brothels that were located here.

Stop 8

You have arrived at Pye Corner, the point where the Fire is supposed to have stopped and our last stop. Look up and you will see the statue of the Golden Boy erected 'in Memory put up for the late Fire of London. Occasion'd by the sin of Gluttony.' The Fire had started in Pudding Lane and ended at Pye Corner so, Londoners reasoned, it must have been God's punishment for Greed. This made about as much sense as blaming the Catholics. Neither place had much to do with food. Pudding Lane was named after the entrails left on

the streets from butchered animals while Pye Corner was named after its resident magpies.

Before we leave take a look at the inscription below the Golden Boy. It marks the spot of an old pub, The Fortune of War. This was where surgeons from Bart's Hospital pursuing the new science of anatomy would come to buy corpses brought by body snatchers. The bodies would be carefully arranged on benches by the publican for inspection. Clearly the watch house we saw earlier was no great deterrent.

The Great Fire was a turning point for London, marking a key transition to the modern world. As can be seen, there was much to do before it could be called civilised.

Finally

There are some excellent cafes, pubs and restaurants in Smithfield, just keep walking down Giltspur Street. The nearest Underground is St. Paul's. Retrace your steps to Newgate Street and turn left.

Greenwich: Wren's Vision for London

We have seen how, after the Great Fire, London was rebuilt on its old medieval street plan despite the best endeavours of Christopher Wren. There was one part of London though where his vision and genius were allowed free rein – Greenwich. He and his associates, especially his apprentice, Nicholas Hawksmoor, transformed the village and turned it into a grand symbol of the new age of enlightenment. We are going to head out to South East London to understand the intellectual climate of the end of the seventeenth century.

Greenwich has always been separate from London with its hill overlooking the Thames and dominating the approach to the City. Today, it is one of the great tourist attractions of England but its history goes back to at least Roman times. The old road from Kent and the Continent runs across Blackheath at the top of Greenwich Hill and a Roman temple has been found in the Park. The Anglo-Saxons settled here and named it: Greenwich, the Green Village. It was here that the invading Vikings in 1012 brought the Archbishop of Canterbury, Alfege, to London as a captive to bargain for ransom. When Alfege refused to be ransomed the drunken Vikings beat him to death using ox bones. Greenwich's parish church was built on the site of his martyrdom and became a shrine for pilgrims. For the next four hundred years, Greenwich remained a small and peaceful fishing village on the banks of the Thames but its fortunes were about to change.

In 1447, a royal palace was built by the riverside and enclosed the great sweep of the hill as its hunting park. By the start of the sixteenth century, it was known as the Palace of Placentia, meaning Pleasure, and had become one of the favourite palaces of the Tudor monarchs. It was the birthplace of Henry VIII as well as his two daughters Mary and Elizabeth. By the middle of the century, it had become one of the country's great royal palaces comparable to Hampton Court 20 miles upstream. In 1616 James I had the revolutionary Queen's House the first classical building in Britain built for his wife, Anne of Denmark, by Inigo Jones. Under Charles's rule, however, Greenwich became less popular and the Palace increasingly run down. During the Civil War it suffered the ignominy of becoming a biscuit factory and a prisoner of war camp for Parliament to house captured Royalists.

At the Restoration of 1660, Charles II decided to rebuild the Palace in the grand classical style and commissioned John Webb as the architect. The project was taken over by Christopher Wren who transformed the medieval palace into the great statement of neo-classical architecture that we see today. The view from the river is world-famous, protected by law and painted by Canaletto but it also represents a new vision of the world: it is ordered, rational and logical. Gone are the nooks and crannies, the foibles of the medieval and Tudor age. All is straight lines and symmetry borrowed and adapted via Italy from the classical world. However, the view comes to us almost by accident as the then owner of the Queen's House, Mary II, insisted on the plans being changed so that she could retain her view of the river.

Our view extends to the Royal Observatory built on the foundations of the medieval tower at the top of the hill. This was also designed by Christopher Wren and is the first purpose built research establishment anywhere in Britain. It became one of the centres of the scientific revolution of the last half of the seventeenth century. The observatory's aim was to measure the heavens 'so as to find out the much desired longitude of places for the perfecting of the art of navigation'. Thus the link between scientific investigation and British maritime power was forged. The search for an accurate measure of longitude was only finally solved a hundred years after the foundation of the Observatory with the development of John Harrison's marine clock. The wait was worthwhile for the benefits of such precise navigation were enormous. British ships could accurately determine where they were anywhere in the world; an essential condition for trade and for empire. For the clock to work an agreed base time was needed and so Greenwich Mean Time was born, first as the basis of English time and later, after international agreement in 1884, of world time. The measurement of time has now gone sub-atomic but the legacy of Greenwich remains. Each day at 1 pm precisely a great red ball descends from the roof of the observatory. This was used by ships' captains to set their chronometers.

The new royal palace at Greenwich was never used for its original purpose of a royal residence. By the time it was completed the eastern edge of London was no longer so attractive with the spread of industry along the river. Kensington, St James's and Whitehall palaces were much more to the tastes of successive monarchs. The Palace at Greenwich was turned into the Royal Naval Hospital, a match for the army's facility at Chelsea. The hospital must have made a remarkable impact in the eighteenth century; after all, sailors were the lowest of the low needing a press-gang to force them into the navy. Yet, the wounded, injured and sick of these unfortunates were housed and treated in one of the greatest buildings in England.

As Britain rose to rule the waves in the nineteenth century the bloody sea battles declined and so the need for the hospital fell and in 1873 it became the Royal Naval College and for over a hundred years it trained the officers of the Royal Navy. Its latest use is as the home of the University of Greenwich and the Trinity Laban Conservatoire.

There is still more history to Greenwich. Hawksmoor rebuilt St. Alfege in his English Baroque style, sweeping Georgian terraces and squares were built to rival those of Islington and the West End. Even its railway station is historic; it's reputedly the world's oldest passenger station.

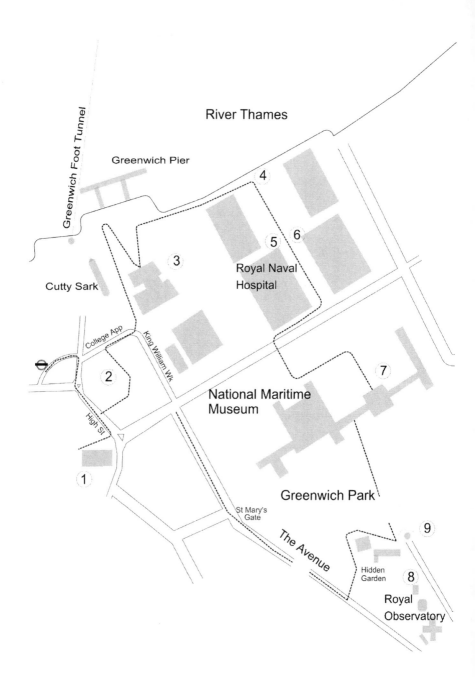

River Thames

Greenwich Foot Tunnel

Greenwich Pier

Cutty Sark

College App

King William Wk.

High St.

Royal Naval Hospital

National Maritime Museum

Greenwich Park

St Mary's Gate

The Avenue

Hidden Garden

Royal Observatory

3

4

5

6

7

1

2

8

9

A Walk through Christopher Wren's Greenwich

There is so much to do in Greenwich; just visiting the museums would easily take up at a day or two and the park on a sunny day is a delight. In this walk we explore Greenwich and in particular we see how it rejected older styles of architecture and became one of the centres of the English Enlightenment, embracing science, mathematics, logic and order. We will see how great architects like Inigo Jones, Christopher Wren and Nicholas Hawksmoor decisively broke with past styles and laid down the blueprint for a new London.

This walk starts at Cutty Sark Station on Docklands Light Railway and can finish at the same location, Greenwich Main Line Station or the Clipper Pier.

Details of what you'll see on this walk start on the page which follows this map...

1 St Alfege Church

2 Greenwich Market

3 Visitor Centre

4 Royal Naval College

5 Painted Hall

6 Chapel of Royal College

7 Queen's House

8 Royal Observatory

9 General Wolfe Statue

Come out of the Cutty Sark Station, turn left down the passage way, right on to the high street and walk up the road. You arrive at St. Alfege's, the parish church of Greenwich. The entrance is down a small passageway just before you reach the great bulk of the church. The main door is at what seems to be the back of the church, set in a peaceful little square, a million miles away from the bustle of tourist Greenwich.

Stop 1

St. Alfege is one of the great churches of London. It was built on the site where Vikings murdered Alfege, the Archbishop of Canterbury in 1012, and it became a place of pilgrimage. It reached its heyday in Tudor times as it was the nearest church to the great Palace of Greenwich. Henry VIII was baptised here and General James Wolfe, one of England's great military heroes, was buried here. They and other notables are commemorated in the stained glass windows in the church.

A church has been on this site for almost a thousand years but the present church was built in 1718 and is the work of Nicholas Hawksmoor, one of the greatest British architects and pupil of Sir Christopher Wren. Hawksmoor worked with Wren on some of the greatest projects of the time: the Chelsea Hospital, St. Paul's and the Greenwich Naval Hospital. St. Alfege was Hawksmoor's first church and he went on to design a further five in London as part of Queen Anne's Act to provide 50 new churches in London. It is seen as one of the great masterpieces of the new English Baroque style reflecting Hawksmoor's emphasis on solidity, exuberance and style.

Inside, the church is a jewel. It was badly damaged in the Blitz but was faithfully restored and is now a beautiful example of an early eighteenth century church. The church is famous for its music recitals, quite appropriate given that it's the resting place of Thomas Tallis, court composer to four monarchs: Henry VIII, Edward VI, Mary I and Elizabeth I.

Leave the church the way you came looking at the beautiful early nineteenth century houses that surround the square. Just to the left diagonally across the main road you will see a small passage leading into Greenwich Market. Walk down the alley and into the market.

Stop 2

This fine building dates from 1737 and is now full of stalls selling antiques, craft, art and food from around the world. As you exit through the main entrance on to College Approach note the stern injunction 'A False Balance is an Abomination to the Lord but a just weight is his delight'.

Turn right down College Approach, left down King William Walk and past the Cutty Sark. The Cutty Sark Museum is well worth a visit, especially with children, although a terrible fire destroyed much of the original ship in 2007. At the end of the nineteenth century it was one of the fastest ships in the world and specialised first as a tea clipper then in importing Australian wool.

Walk beyond the Cutty Sark to the riverside, noting the entrance to the Greenwich Foot Tunnel. This was built in 1902 to enable dockers living in Greenwich easy access to the great West India docks. At the river bank turn right and you reach on your right the main entrance of the Visitor Centre.

Stop 3

The Visitor Centre introduces you to the many glories of Greenwich but it concentrates on the historic riverside. This was where Henry VII built the Palace of Placentia or Pleasure, the great summer palace of the Tudor kings and queens. The centre documents its rebuilding by Christopher Wren and others to become the Royal Hospital for Seamen at Greenwich, then the Royal Naval College and today the home of the University of Greenwich and the Trinity Laban Conservatoire. It is worth spending a little time here to see what the old Tudor Palace looked like and how it contrasts with Wren's new palace. The museum also describes how the Hospital functioned when it was full of wounded sailors.

Walk back to the riverside and walk along to the grand Water Gate, the riverside entrance to the complex.

Stop 4

The view before you has been described by UNESCO as the 'finest and most dramatically sited architectural and landscape ensemble in the British Isles'.

You are enclosed by Christopher Wren's great ensemble of royal

buildings which perfectly frame the Queen's House. All is symmetry with the Chapel on the left facing the great Painted Hall on your right. Only one building is slightly awry. On the brow of the hill the Greenwich Observatory also built by Wren lies off to the right. Now Wren was a master of symmetry so why is his Observatory askew? The reason as so often was about money: the Observatory was built on the existing foundations of the original Greenwich castle to cut costs.

Stop 5

You are surrounded by wonders: in front of you to the right is the Painted Hall 'Britain's Sistine Chapel' as the Greenwich Tourist Office label it. The enormous painting on the ceiling is certainly pretty magnificent even if you don't think Sir James Thornhill who painted it in 1726 is quite as good an artist as Michelangelo. It covers nearly 4,000 square metres so there's certainly quantity even if the quality is not quite that of the Sistine Chapel. It is certainly worth considering paying the somewhat steep admission charge if only to stand in the spot where Nelson lay in state after his death at Trafalgar.

Stop 6

Opposite the Painted Hall is the Chapel of the Royal Hospital which is almost as spectacular as the Hall but free to all. While the chapel is contemporaneous with the rest of the Hospital and designed by Wren, it had to be rebuilt after a devastating fire in 1779. Today it is a beautiful building containing memorials to many of the greatest heroes of the Royal Navy. Look out for the one to Thomas Hardy (as in Nelson's last words 'Kiss me Hardy').

Walk between the Painted Hall and the Chapel and bear right to exit the complex and cross the road to make your way towards the Queen's House framed between the two wings of the Hospital.

Stop 7

This has been called the most important house in Britain as it was the first building to break decisively with the whimsical native Tudor architecture and adopt the remorseless classicism of the Palladian revolution. The architect, Inigo Jones, captured the essence of Palladio to perfection and the house's symmetry and style became the blue print for the Georgian houses of the next two hundred years.

It was built originally for the wife of James I in 1616. The legend goes that James built it for Ann of Denmark as an apology for shouting at her after she had shot his dog during a hunting accident. Not a bad pay off for a marital tiff. The house was only finally completed in 1635 and Wren was forced to change his designs for the Royal Palace due to the insistence of the new queen that her river view should not be impeded.

As beautiful as the building is outside, its real treasures are inside. It houses a wonderful gallery of maritime, royal and landscape art. Highlights include works by Lowry, Turner and Canaletto and the wonderful Armada portrait of Elizabeth I. Architecturally, there are also wonders. The main hall is a perfect cube with a beautiful view of the river; the

Tulip Stairs were an innovation, the first self supporting stairs in the UK and the building itself spans the old road to Woolwich. It's worth exploring as it's one of the great, unknown galleries of London.

When you're finished with the Queen's House, walk through the colonnade to the right of the house to a gate at the back. In front of you stretches Greenwich Park, perhaps the most beautiful park in London.

There is much to see and do here. You could walk to your left and follow paths around the edge of the Park to the top. Amongst other delights you will see the entrances to Tudor tunnels built into the side of the hill which brought water to the palace, the remnants of a Roman camp or temple and a deer park at the top of the hill the inhabitants of which are thought to be descended from those who survived Henry VIII's attempts to massacre them. Above all there are beautiful and spectacular gardens to admire before descending to the Observatory.

If time is short or the weather not great, bear right and walk up the hill towards the Observatory on its brow. Whichever way you go, it's a stiff climb especially as you reach the top.

Stop 8

The observatory was designed by Wren in 1675 but in a very different fashion to the baroque glories of the Naval Hospital below. In comparison it is positively homely, built in a warm, red brick. The Observatory was the first dedicated scientific establishment in the United Kingdom and played a major role in plotting the movements of the heavens. It played a critical role in helping establish the tools of navigation, including the development of very accurate clocks to determine longitude. Inside the Observatory for the payment of a pretty hefty admission charge there is a wealth of information about astronomy and navigation. Most famously, there is the brass strip in the ground which is the line separating the eastern and western hemispheres where thousands of tourists have had their photos taken as they straddled East and West. It is from this point that Greenwich Mean Time is measured as it is exactly 12 noon GMT when the sun crosses this line. At 1pm precisely every day a red ball is dropped down a post on the roof of the observatory. The reason that it was dropped at 1 rather than 12 was that the astronomers were too busy checking the sun's position to worry about the ball so gave themselves an hour to get sorted.

There is still much to do in and around the Royal Observatory even if you don't pay the entry charge. Just south of the Observatory is a cafe and an educational centre which hosts free exhibitions on space. In its entrance you can touch a meteorite 4.5 billion years old and inside they often have stunning photographs of deep space.

There are also two places where you can stand astride the meridian line, this time for free. One is in the gardens at the back of the observatory where a black line runs down the side of the building and across the path. The other we'll meet on the way down.

Once you have finished exploring, leave the complex at the gate on the side and walk to the statue of General James Wolfe at the very top of the hill.

Stop 9

This is one of the greatest views of London. Beneath you is the Queen's House, the Naval Hospital and then, across the river, Canary Wharf. To your left the City of London is spread out before you including a glimpse of St. Paul's Cathedral.

James Wolfe was one of the military heroes of eighteenth century Britain. His defeat of the French at the battle of Quebec of 1759 effectively ensured that Canada became part of the British Empire. He died there but is buried in St. Alfege Church in Greenwich. You'll see that his statue has been damaged; this time by a bomb during the Second World War.

Walk down the narrow footpath skirting the north wall of the Observatory and entered through a kissing gate. Here you will find the second place where you can straddle the hemispheres; a stone plaque with a brass line crossing the path.

Follow this path down past beautiful hidden gardens until you meet the main drive through the park and walk down through the main gates. If you have time you could now visit the National Maritime Museum with its wonderful collection of memorabilia tracing the course of British naval history over the last 500 years.

Otherwise find your way to the town centre with its pubs and restaurants, some overlooking the river.

Finally

To get back to Central London, you can take the mainline services to London Bridge, the Docklands Light Railway to Canary Wharf or even the Clipper along the Thames to Embankment. You could follow the Thames Path for a kilometre or so eastwards from the town centre, past the University of Greenwich where you walk past some beautiful almshouses and then come to the Cutty Sark, a really great pub.

Doctor Johnson's London

London in the mid-eighteenth century had recovered fully from the Great Fire of 1666 and was one of the biggest and richest cities in the world. It had shrugged off its medieval roots and was now reinventing itself as a recognisably modern city. As a result, it was in intellectual ferment. In literature, Daniel Defoe had published the first recognisably modern novel in Robinson Crusoe. In the theatre, David Garrick was transforming the art of acting. Alexander Pope observed with a caustic eye the salons of London poking fun at the pretensions of the time. William Hogarth captured the cruelty and injustices of society in a series of coruscating images of London life such as Gin Lane or the Rake's Progress. In philosophy, Edmund Burke and David Hume were developing a recognisably British philosophical tradition. The first newspapers were being printed with an eager readership as literacy spread. Even more popular were the lurid pamphlets of the time such as the Newgate Chronicles which detailed the last hours of those being executed at Tyburn. In the coffee houses, trading deals were being struck which were both generating wealth and turning those same houses into business institutions.

At the heart of this intellectual life was the towering figure of Samuel Johnson. His life had started inauspiciously. Born in Litchfield, he had suffered from scrofula, the King's Evil, so called because it was thought that a touch from the King was its only cure. In fact it is a form of TB leading to scarring and despite the infant Samuel being 'touched' by Queen Anne, he remained disfigured. He also probably had a form of Tourette's as he was given to violent tics and gesticulations. His father, a bookseller, had gone bankrupt leaving Johnson unable to complete his degree at Oxford. Johnson had started life as a very unsuccessful school teacher, had married a woman twenty years his senior and wasted her money on setting up his own school which failed soon after. He then left her in the Midlands to make his fortune in London accompanied by one of his students, the young David Garrick.

In London, after some very hard years Johnson eventually flourished and was able to bring his wife to stay with him. His name was made when he was commissioned to create an authoritative dictionary of the English Language. Whilst it was not the first, it became the most used until the creation of the Oxford English Dictionary 150 years later. As a result Dr Johnson has been seen as the 'father of the English language' as for the first time English itself became the subject of study with accepted spellings and rules for grammar. Johnson also wrote the first recognisably modern biography, the first theatre criticism as well as journalism, essays and poetry. He transformed the study of Shakespeare when he reissued all of his plays with annotations explaining the meaning hidden within them.

Above all Samuel Johnson was at the heart of intellectual life in the capital. In 1763, he formed 'The Club', a group of friends who met regularly to discuss the issues of the day. They included David Garrick, Joshua Reynolds, James Boswell, Edmund Burke, Oliver Goldsmith, Adam Smith and Charles James Fox. Its presiding genius was Johnson whose spirit was captured in Boswell's biography.

The geographical centre of this ferment was the area around Fleet Street. Fleet Street had been the main route out of London to the west since Roman times. Historically it linked the two great centres of London: political and monarchical power based in Westminster and economic wealth of the City and the ecclesiastical authority of the Cathedral. In medieval times it led past the best real estate in London. The Templars had their headquarters here which eventually became the Middle and Inner Temple, the centre of law, home of lawyers and generating vast amounts of written material every year. Along the river as far as Westminster, the Thames was lined by the houses of the great nobles.

It was because of this location that for 500 years the publishing industry was based in this area. It was first begun by the wonderfully named Wynkyn de Worde, a partner of William Caxton. In 1500, he set up a printshop on Ludgate Hill. Two hundred years later, the first British daily paper, the Daily Courant was published just by Fleet Bridge. Remarkably its first editor was a woman, Elizabeth Mallet. By the beginning of the twentieth century Fleet Street was the hub of the newspaper industry in Britain with the new mass circulation titles, the Mail, Express and Mirror competing with older, more venerable papers like the Times, Observer and Telegraph. All were based in or around Fleet Street until the technological revolution of the late twentieth century swept the industry away, first to Docklands and then scattered across the country.

While Fleet Street remains a busy thoroughfare, often congested and always polluted, the alleyways on either side are a delight, quiet, traffic free and full of reminders of a past age. They include beautiful houses dating back to the time of Dr Johnson and before.

As Dr Johnson himself said:

'If you wish to have a just notion of the magnitude of this city, you must not be satisfied with seeing its great streets and squares but must survey the innumerable little lanes and courts. It is not in the showy evolutions of buildings, but in the multiplicity of human habitations which are crowded together, that the wonderful immensity of London consists'.

And it is this immensity that we will explore on our walk.

A Walk through Dr Johnson's London

In this walk, we follow in the footsteps of Samuel Johnson through the 'innumerable little lanes and courts' which lie, often almost unknown, behind some of the busiest streets in London. We will see where he lived, worked and entertained his friends in the heart of eighteenth century London.

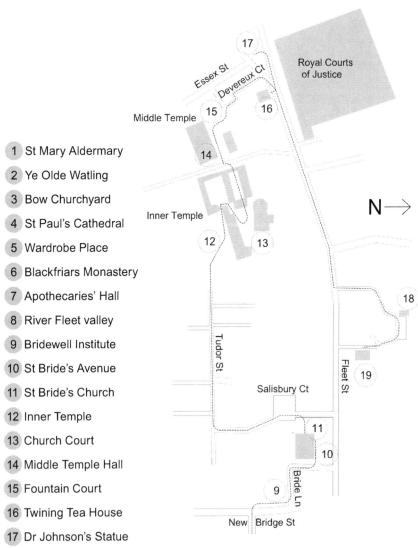

1 St Mary Aldermary

2 Ye Olde Watling

3 Bow Churchyard

4 St Paul's Cathedral

5 Wardrobe Place

6 Blackfriars Monastery

7 Apothecaries' Hall

8 River Fleet valley

9 Bridewell Institute

10 St Bride's Avenue

11 St Bride's Church

12 Inner Temple

13 Church Court

14 Middle Temple Hall

15 Fountain Court

16 Twining Tea House

17 Dr Johnson's Statue

18 Dr Johnson's House

19 Ye Olde Cheshire Cheese

This walk starts at Mansion House Tube Station and finishes at Fleet Street; nearest stations Blackfriars, Thameslink or St. Paul's.

Stop 1

Come out of Mansion House Station and in front of you, you will see a great church tower. This is your first stop. Walk up Bow Lane and on your right you pass the wonderful Wren church of St Mary Aldermary Church. Make sure you go inside as it hosts an excellent cafe selling good coffee which supports local charities. The church itself is magnificent with the most beautiful plaster vaulting on the ceiling. One element strikes a discordant note, look carefully at the wall behind the altar and you notice the wall is askew and not at right angles to the nave. The reason can be seen outside the church: a medieval alley runs at the back of the church and Wren had to find an ingenious way of building a new church on a much older site. Exit the church on to Watling Street.

To your right you will see a statue of a shoe maker, there because the church is in the ancient Ward of Cordwainer. The word means shoemaker and until quite recently there was a Cordwainer College in London. It is derived from Cordoba, the Spanish city from where the finest leather came.

Turn left down Watling Street. This is one of the most ancient and historic roads in Britain. Parts of it were probably old before the Romans came but they turned it into one of their great military roads stretching from Dover to Anglesey. The London leg that we are standing on links London Bridge to St Paul's and then onwards to Newgate and the north west.

Stop 2

At the corner with Bow Lane, have a look at the pub Ye Olde Watling. This claims to be one of the oldest pubs in the city, built by Wren for the construction workers building St. Paul's nearby. It is certainly very old. You will notice the window frames are flush to the walls and not inset. This dates the building to before the 1750s after that date all windows had to be set back as a fire precaution.

Turn right down Bow Lane, noting the 'innumerable little lanes' running off to the right. Turn down Groveland Court, a blind alley on your left. At the end you notice a beautiful late seventeenth century town house. This was the home of the Lord Mayor of London until it was decided that the top official of such an important city needed something a bit more impressive and the grandiose Mansion House was built to replace it in the 1740s. Notice the fine gates in front of the house; a gift from William and Mary to the city on their accession after the Glorious Revolution of 1688. Their initials can be seen in the ironwork.

Retrace your steps and continue walking up Bow Lane for a few metres and then turn left into Bow Churchyard.

Stop 3

In the centre of the churchyard is a fine statue of Captain John Smith. He was born nearby and was a cordwainer but went on to become Governor of the state of Virginia where his life was famously saved by Pocahontas.

St Mary-le-Bow has been regarded over the years as the greatest church in the City of London after St. Paul's. Called le-Bow after the rounded shape of the windows in the crypt, it houses the Bow Bell; if you are born within the sound of it you can call yourself a Cockney. This was because its great bell used to ring out the curfew at 9 pm each day in medieval London. It was also the bell that supposedly called Dick Whittington back to London where he was to become London's most famous Mayor.

There has been a church on the site for a thousand years or more with the original possibly being Saxon. However, it rose to fame after the Norman Conquest as being the base for the Archbishop of Canterbury in London who held his legal and ecclesiastical hearings in the church. You can still enter the tiny crypt down the stairs which lead from the churchyard. This is one of the oldest rooms in London still being regularly used.

The main body of the church was rebuilt by Wren after the Great Fire and then had to be completely restored after being badly damaged in the Blitz. Despite this, it remains a very beautiful church.

It faces on to Cheapside, one of the widest streets in London, much wider than the alleys we have been passing through. This is because it was the principal market street in medieval London. Indeed the word 'cheap' means market in early English. Many of the small streets that lead off it; Milk, Wood, Bread Streets, Poultry and Honey Lane, remind us what used to be sold there. Cheapside was also used as a royal processional route and for jousting. If you look up at the tower of the church you will see there is a balcony looking over Cheapside. This commemorates the balcony used by royalty 700 years ago to watch the tournaments below. Famously, it collapsed whilst Philippa, Queen of Edward III, was watching a joust below. The balcony was rebuilt and remains to remind us of those events.

Walk down Cheapside and then turn left into Bread Street, noticing the plaque marking the birth place of John Milton, the poet and Oliver Cromwell's Foreign Secretary. Walk through New Change, a modern shopping centre, saved from banality by the stupendous view of the back of St. Paul's.

Stop 4

Walk to the left through the Churchyard of St. Paul's. The streets around you were the centre of ecclesiastical power for centuries and the centre of the book publishing trade. The names of the roads bear this out. There are streets called Friar, Creed, Pilgrim, Ave Maria, Paternoster and Amen and the Stationers Guild Hall is just by Ludgate Hill.

Cross over to the aptly named Godliman Street and walk right down Carter Lane. This dates back to the early thirteenth century and was perhaps London's first bypass aiming to take the noisy carts away from St. Paul's Cathedral to avoid disturbing the services.

Stop outside the spectacular Youth Hostel, enjoying perhaps the best location for a hostel anywhere in Britain. It is housed in what used to be the school for the choristers of St. Paul's. Built in the 1870s, its facade is covered in Victorian Latin inscriptions. A few metres further down Carter Lane on your left you go through a small gate way into Wardrobe Place.

Stop 5

Wardrobe Place is a beautiful little square with some enormous London plane trees. The buildings here on the right date from shortly after the Great Fire. Its name reminds us that this was the site where the Crown kept many of its household goods like furniture, uniforms and tapestries from 1381 until the Fire.

Leave Wardrobe Place and then walk down St Andrew's Hill until you reach a pub, the Cockpit, on your right. Its name refers to the 'pastime' of cock fighting which was big entertainment for our forebears.

Stop 6

You are now standing at the entrance to the great monastery of Blackfriars that was based in this area from 1278. Run by the Dominicans (derived from Domini Cani, Dogs of the Lord) this was one of the biggest monasteries in London. It hosted the divorce proceedings of Henry VIII and Catherine of Aragon which eventually led to its dissolution and destruction. Part of the monastery was converted into a playhouse by James Burbage and used by the troupe 'The King's Men'. Shakespeare was a leading playwright and actor in this company and as a result he bought himself a lodging within the old gatehouse to the monastery, a fact commemorated on a wall plaque.

Walk down through Ireland Yard and you will pass the graveyard of St. Ann's. It's a quiet spot and holds the only existing part of the great Blackfriars monastery: a small and unimpressive broken wall.

Further down Ireland Yard you come to Church Entry, with yet another peaceful and secluded graveyard.

Retrace your steps and carry on walking down Ireland Yard. You enter Playhouse Yard, the site of Burbage's theatre which lasted until it was closed by Cromwell and demolished after the Civil War.

Walk across the Yard and turn right up Blackfriars Lane.

Stop 7

On your right you see the entrance to Apothecaries' Hall and you can walk into its beautiful courtyard rebuilt shortly after the Fire. The Apothecaries were one of the great medieval livery companies. They were concerned with the development and production of medicines and are still involved in specialist courses for medical practitioners. Notice its great crest with unicorns surmounted by a surprised looking rhinoceros. Clearly the misplaced belief in the magical powers of a rhino's horn has a long history.

Walk up the stairs behind you across the pedestrian bridge which takes you over the Thameslink railway line. In front of you the ground drops away as this is the valley of the River Fleet.

Stop 8

The Fleet is the largest and longest of London's hidden rivers. It rises on Hampstead Heath and flows down through Camden Town, Kings Cross, Holborn and Farringdon Road before entering the Thames at Blackfriars Bridge. For many years it was where London's coal was unloaded as the names Seacoal and Newcastle Lane remind us. As time progressed, the Fleet became increasingly filthy, being used as an open sewer. Its banks were lined with undesirable places: the abattoir of Smithfield, the slums of Saffron Hill, the prisons of Newgate, Fleet, Bridewell and Ludgate.

The river was gradually covered over from the 1730s on and now is used to flush the sewers of London.

From your vantage point on top of the bridge you can see across the Fleet valley an entrance to a grand building normally flying a Union Jack flag. Above the entrance a head is carved into the portico. It is a bust of Edward VI and it marks the site of Bridewell Palace. This was one of the preferred homes of his father, Henry VIII. Edward gave the palace to the City of London who used it as an orphanage and reform school. Over the years it increasingly specialised in the punishment of 'disorderly women' and the weekly whippings became a popular attraction along with visits to see the mentally ill in its sister institution of the Bethlehem Hospital (aka Bedlam) in the late eighteenth century. The name Bridewell is still used to mean a gaol or lockup.

Descend into the valley, cross New Bridge Street and walk right until you turn left into Bride Lane.

Stop 9

Walk past the Bridewell Institute, a late Victorian Institution set up to bring learning into the City. Follow the Lane as it bends to the right and then go up the steps to the left of the pub along St. Bride's Avenue.

Stop 10

You are standing between Fleet Street and the courtyard of St Brides Church. The art deco black and chrome building behind you used to be the offices of the Daily Express while the imposing building with its ornate clock a few doors down on the left was that of the Daily Telegraph.

The name Bridewell comes from St. Bridget's Well. She was an Irish nun, long associated with springs and water and is said to have built this church on Roman foundations. It is extraordinarily old with Roman, Saxon and Medieval remains. In the courtyard, King John held a parliament with his rebellious barons before signing the Magna Carta. Destroyed in the Great Fire, it was rebuilt by Wren and seen as his greatest parish church. It is certainly his highest; its tower rises 70 metres overlooked in London only by the dome of St. Paul's Cathedral. Famously, it became the model for wedding cakes everywhere after a baker in Ludgate Hill started selling cakes based on its distinctive shape.

Stop 11

The interior of the church is gorgeous though heavily restored after bomb damage during the Blitz. Called the Journalists' Church the seats and walls are lined with memorials to those who worked in the area. In the body of the church is a memorial to Wynkyn de Worde, who began the tradition of printing in Fleet Street. It is worthwhile having a look at the great statues behind the altar, which turn out to be trompe l'oeil and finding a Grinling Gibbons font cover.

The real treasures however are below the church in the crypt. Here you will see a Roman pavement,

Saxon remains, a medieval chapel, remnants of the Great Fire and an exhibition detailing the history of the Church and Fleet Street including the contribution of Dr. Johnson. It is well worth spending some time here.

Exit the church through its central door and turn left into Salisbury Court which turns into Dorset Rise, the names reminding us that the aristocracy used these prime lands sloping down to the Thames as their London houses. At the bottom turn right down Tudor Street, passing Whitefriars and Carmelite Streets. These remember the time when this area was part of the Whitefriars monastery just across the Fleet from Blackfriars.

After the dissolution it became a place of great ill-repute, nicknamed Alsatia, after Alsace then seen as a wild frontier region. Alsatia lay outside the normal rule of law and had rights of sanctuary for criminals, a right only abolished in 1697. Today it is much more respectable if a little soulless.

Go through the gate in front of you into the calm of the Inner Temple.

Stop 12

You are now in the Inner Temple, one of the four great Inns of Court, with its symbol, Pegasus, the flying horse all around you. The four Inns of Court (Inner Temple, Middle Temple, Lincoln's Inn and Gray's Inn) are associations for the training of barristers and every barrister belongs to one of them. Each Inn provides training with a library, hall and chapel as well as accommodation for lawyers, their clerks and judges.

The history of the Temple lands stretches back nine hundred years. They originally belonged to the Knights Templar, a military order set up in 1119 to defend pilgrims and Crusaders on their way to Jerusalem. The Templars began to develop some legal expertise as they would often be tasked to administer wills of those who did not return. After the fall of Jerusalem in the thirteenth century, the fighting Templars whilst rich were no longer required and they were suppressed, bloodily in France in 1314 and, more politely, in England a few years later. Their London lands were given to another catholic order, the St. John Hospitallers who had provided medical services to pilgrims.

During the fourteenth century lawyers began to congregate within the Temple area and its reputation as a place of learning for lawyers grew so that by the fifteenth century the four Inns were recognised as the centre of the legal profession. When the monasteries were suppressed in 1538 the Temple land was eventually given to the lawyers who lived and worked there.

The Inner Temple where you are standing was almost completely destroyed by the Great Fire and the Kings Bench buildings are some of the earliest rebuilds in London. The insides of the doors carry lists of the lawyers and judges who inhabit the chambers, some have permanent accommodation there.

Walk across the square keeping to the left of the modern hall of the Inner Temple; walk through the small alleyway and you are in Elm Court, a hidden oasis, with the only surviving secular part of the original

Templar buildings. This is the Buttery or Pantry. Follow the building and you arrive in Church Court, the most historic part of the Temple.

Stop 13

Church Court contains a single church built in two very different styles. On the left is the original Temple church. Built in 1185, it is Romanesque with distinctive bowed window arches. It is round because it is modelled on the Church of the Holy Sepulchre in Jerusalem. Inside are the tombs of some of the great Templar knights, including William Marshall, key mover in forcing King John to sign the Magna Carta. These have made the church internationally famous after its starring role in 'The Da Vinci Code'.

Such was the prestige of the Templars that in 1240, Henry III expressed a wish to be buried in the church. To prepare for this, it was significantly enlarged with the addition of a new nave built in Early English style and this is the part of the church to your right, recognisable by the pointed windows. In the event, Henry III was buried in Westminster Abbey but the church remains.

Also in the square is the memorial to the Templars. Note that there are two knights looking a little uncomfortable, squeezed onto a single horse. This is because they took a vow of poverty and had to share the horse between them.

Walk round to the left hand side of the church where you can see the oldest part of the structure without the Victorian restoration. Note the very old carvings surrounding the main entrance. Just behind you is a sign proclaiming Johnson's Buildings as the Doctor lived here for a while.

Walk into Pump Court through the arcade at the west end of Church Court. You are now in the Middle Temple and you will see its symbol, the Lamb of God - Agnus Dei, at every turn. At the end of the court turn left.

Stop 14

You are now facing Middle Temple's Elizabethan Great Hall, the finest Tudor building in the City of London. Built in 1572, and patronised by Queen Elizabeth I it has a wonderful hammer beam roof and portraits of Tudor and Stuart monarchs. When students are called to the bar to become barristers, they  sign on a table made out of the hatch of the Golden Hind, the ship in which Sir Francis Drake circumnavigated the globe. It also hosted the world premiere of Twelfth Night in 1602 almost certainly in the presence of Shakespeare. The easiest way of seeing the gorgeous interior is to book lunch there.

Stop 15

To the right of the Hall is the beautiful Fountain Court. Mentioned by Dickens in Martin Chuzzlewhit, it is one of the most beautiful and tranquil places in the heart of London. To the south the gardens of the Middle Temple sweep down to the Thames. According to Shake-

speare, this is where Yorkists and Lancastrians plucked the white and red roses initiating the start of the Wars of the Roses. To the north, there is a sign pointing to Essex Street and legal offices called Devereux Chambers. This marks the area where Robert Devereux, Earl of Essex and rumoured lover of Elizabeth I had his great London mansion. When she spurned his advances, he rose in revolt only to end on the execution spot on Tower Hill. He's remembered by a bust looking down Essex Street and painted a lurid red.

In the middle of the square you see two old houses facing each other and built just after the Great Fire dated of 1667 and 1677. These were built by Nicholas Barbon, the first modern speculative builder. He was the son of an ex-speaker of the House of Commons who gave his name to the 'Barebones Parliament' of Oliver Cromwell. He was a strong puritan and had given his son the catchy middle name of 'If-Jesus-Christ-had-not-died-for-thee-thou-hadst-been-damned'. The sentiment didn't seem to steer his son in a particularly moral direction, however. He was notorious for ignoring planning constraints and throwing up large estates of houses, sometimes poorly built on inadequate foundations. Whatever his faults elsewhere, the houses in front of us seem both sturdy and elegant.

Go out of the gates and right through Essex Street. This was the site of one of the most famous 'Molly Houses' in London. These were clubs where gay men could meet and act out their fantasies and desires.

Stop 16

This takes you on to the Strand, a continuation of Fleet Street, opposite the Victorian Gothic Royal Courts of Justice. Just to your right is one of the smallest and quirkiest museums in London based in Twinings Tea House. The store was created by Thomas Twining in 1707 within an existing coffee house but specialised in teas. It was a great success especially amongst women of the upper classes. At the time they were the only ones able to afford the very high prices. Those prices are still reflected in some of the rarest and finest teas that Twinings continue to import which sell for up to £250 a pound. It's well worth a visit especially to the tea bar at the back where the first thing the assistants tell you is not to use boiling water to make a cup of tea!

Cross into the traffic island in the middle of Strand and turn left to the statue of Samuel Johnson.

Stop 17

The statue of Samuel Johnson does manage to convey the power of the man although he could be pretty alarming in the flesh.

Walk eastwards past the Royal Courts of Justice looking out for number 17 Fleet Street, which dates back to 1610, and then St Dunstan's-in-the-West with its bell tower featuring the two mythical giants of London, Gog and Magog, plus London's only statue of Elizabeth I. Enthusiasts will notice the offices of DC Thomson, publishers of the Beano next to the offices of the Protestant Truth Society. Cross Fetter Lane and then turn up the third alley on the left directing you to Johnson's Court. Wind your way through Johnson's 'little lanes', noting a plaque on the wall telling you that Johnson lived in a since demolished house. Finally you arrive in Gough Square.

Stop 18

You have arrived at Dr Johnson's House, a museum dedicated to his life and in which he lived while he worked on the great Dictionary. It is well worth a visit if you're interested in the great man and his friends and acquaintances. They include James Boswell, the writer of Johnson's biography, Francis Barber, a freed slave who became his servant, friend, executor and heir. There is a copy of the dictionary along with many other Johnson works but best of all there is an atmosphere to the house that can transport you back 250 years to another time.

Also in the square, is a monument to Hodge one of Johnson's favourite cats for whom he bought oysters.

Walk past the statue to the right and then take the alley on the left.

Stop 19

You will there find one of London's most iconic pubs: Ye Olde Cheshire Cheese. Rebuilt, it stresses, in 1667, it has an extraordinary literary history. Among the many people who have drank there, apart from Dr Johnson whose local it was for many years, were Oliver Goldsmith, Mark Twain, Tennyson, Conan Doyle, P.G. Wodehouse, Dickens and W.B. Yeats.

This is perhaps as good a place as any to end this walk. As Dr Johnson said: 'There is nothing which has yet been contrived by man, by which so much happiness is produced as by a good tavern'. The Cheese is a very good tavern indeed.

Finally

There are many other places to eat and drink on Fleet Street. Nearest stations are Blackfriars and St. Paul's.

If you're walking between late January and April, you could visit 2 Temple Place, a wonderful museum which used to be owned by William Waldorf Astor, then the richest man in the world or a little further on is Somerset House and the Courtauld Gallery, both always worth a visit.

London's Docks

London has always been a great trading city, its wealth founded by its position on the Thames with its easy access to overseas markets. The Romans had exploited London's position with a thriving dockside around the mouth of the Walbrook. Alfred the Great created a Saxon port at Queenhythe in the City and in the medieval period the river-bank, centred on Billingsgate, was a major port. As London grew so trade became increasingly complex. Monarchs relied on the revenue from tolls imposed on trade for part of their income and, in order, to control trade Elizabeth I created the Legal Quays where all imports had to be unloaded. These Quays stretched only from London Bridge to the Tower, a distance of less than half a mile, and at their centre was Customs House where all duties had to be paid.

The system lasted for 250 years but as trade increased so the Pool of London became over crowded. By the end of the eighteenth century so many ships were moored waiting to unload that it was said that you could walk from London Bridge to Rotherhithe without getting your feet wet just by stepping from one ship to another.

Those ships made a very tempting target for thieves or pirates as they were called at the time. Some commentators estimated that there were 30,000 Londoners 'employed' stealing from ships. Retribution was fierce. Those captured were hung on the river shore at Execution Dock in Wapping. Just to make sure they were actually dead their bodies continued to hang until three tides had passed over them. Finally, the pirates' remains would be tarred and then hung in a gibbet to discourage others. However the pilfering continued despite the bloody punishments. By the end of the eighteenth century the government recognised that major changes were needed to reduce the ship owners' losses and increase the system's efficiency.

In 1800 Robert Milligan, a sugar producer and slave owner, headed a consortium to build the West India Docks. These enormous docks were enclosed by high walls enabling the owners to control who came into the docks and what left them. They were built by a mainly Irish workforce, many of whom stayed on to become dockers. The West India Docks had a monopoly on imports from the Caribbean of sugar, rum and coffee. Other companies followed this example. The East India Company built its docks to the east of the Isle of Dogs at Black-wall. The London Docks followed, completely cutting of the riverside village of Wapping. St Katherine's Dock was built just by the Tower, specialising in high value goods. On the south bank of the Thames the Surrey Docks dealt with the import of timber. Finally, by the middle of the nineteenth century the Victoria and Albert Docks were built. These enormous docks stretched for over three miles and could take the largest ships in the world.

The London riverside was transformed. Wharfs and warehouses lined the Thames on both sides for ten miles downstream from London

Bridge. The river was almost invisible, only reached by the historic 'Stairs' that still remained from medieval times. A typical docklands architecture emerged of platforms, winches and gangways.

Dockland society, too, was transformed. At its peak perhaps 150,000 people were employed in the docks and in associated trades. The East India Company warehouses in Cutler Street alone employed 5,000 porters and clerks. Much of this work, however, was poorly paid and insecure. The docks operated the 'Call On' system, whereby dockers were only employed if a ship arrived. It was the ultimate gig economy. Every morning, hundreds of dockers would mass outside the gates hoping to be chosen for a few hours work. Sometimes the foremen would throw a few tokens into the crowd, watch the fighting and employ those who won. Pay was low, work was insecure and dangerous. The construction of the docks and later the railways destroyed thousands of homes, leading to even greater overcrowding in the slums of the East End.

The poverty of the area along with its role as the point of entry for successive waves of migration led to the rise of industrial and political turmoil. The great Dock Strike of 1889 led to the formation of the mass unions in Britain which dominated labour politics for 100 years. The East End was also the cockpit where radical politics of the communist left and fascist right clashed in the 1930s.

The docks survived the Blitz of 1940 but at a terrible cost. Great swathes of the East End were destroyed by German bombers. Yet the docks recovered and by the 1950s were importing record amounts into London. For 150 years the docks remained at the centre of economic life in London but times were about to change. The advent of containerisation in the 1960s changed the economy of the docks across the world. Suddenly far fewer employees were needed and the priority was for very deep docks to cater for enormous ships and with direct access to the motorway and rail systems. Inner city docks were inefficient and out of date and, one by one, London's great docks began to close and trade switched to deep water ports like Tilbury and Felixstowe. By the end of the 1970s London's docks were derelict.

Over the next twenty years, the London Docklands became the most successful regeneration project in Britain, arguably in the world. Canary Wharf, in the West India Docks, became the financial centre of Europe. Every day some 120,000 workers commute into the Isle of Dogs. The Royal Docks now hosts London City Airport and the ExCel exhibition centre. The Surrey Docks has been transformed into Canada Water, virtually a new town while St Katherine's now delights tourists on summer evenings. Not everyone, of course, benefited from this transformation. Few dockers found employment in the skyscrapers of Canary Wharf and the East End is still home to some of the most concentrated areas of poverty in London.

Today, modernity co-exists with ghostly relics of a past age. Wealth rubs shoulders with deep poverty. Slums have been transformed into highly desirable properties while the river has been opened up with glorious vistas unseen for two hundred years.

A walk through London's docks –
a wander through Wapping

In this walk, we travel down the north bank of the Thames from the Tower of London and eventually to the West India Docks. It passes through a series of individual villages, strung along the north bank of the Thames: Wapping, Shadwell, Radcliffe and Limehouse. This makes it longer than most of the other walks and so I have broken it at Wapping. Part 2 starts where we left at Wapping and ends at Canary Wharf. It could then be extended to the East India Docks and the Royal Docks beyond but that would make it a very long walk indeed.

This walk starts at Tower Hill and finishes at Wapping. *Details of what you'll see on this walk start on the page which follows this map...*

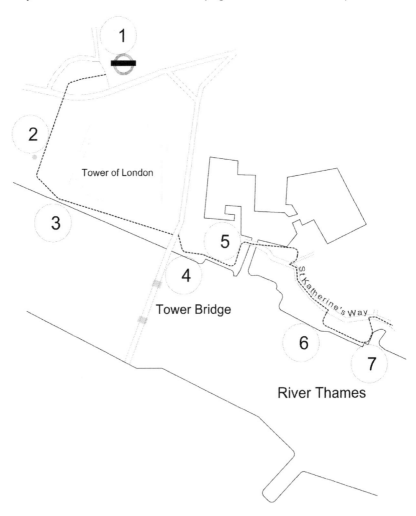

1 Trinity Square
2 London Hydraulic Power Co
3 Pool of London
4 Irongate Wharf
5 St Katherine Dock
6 Alderman Stairs
7 Thames Path
8 Western End of London Docks
9 Western Basin
10 Tobacco Dock
11 St George's
12 Cable Street Mural
13 Raine's School

14 St Peter's, London Docks
15 Turner's Old Star
16 St John's Graveyard and Charity School
17 Pier Head
18 Town of Ramsgate

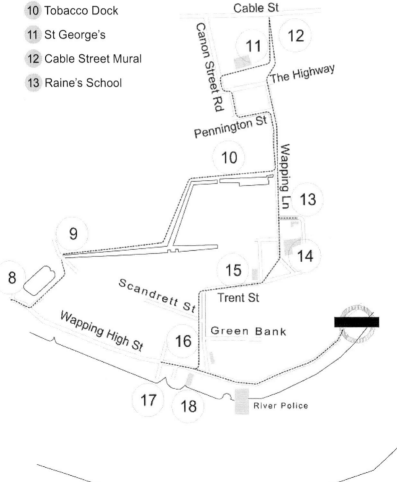

Stop 1

From Tower Hill Underground Station walk into Trinity Square. As we have seen on an earlier walk this is the heart of London's maritime power. To your right is Trinity House, set up by Henry VIII to control the harbours, lighthouses and production of navigational maps. To your left are the monuments to the 50,000 members of the merchant navy that died in two world wars and 'have no grave but the sea'. In front of you, is the gloriously gaudy facade of the old Port of London Authority. Set up in 1909 to administer London's docks it was built on the site of the Navy Board where Samuel Pepys had been employed. At the top of the structure there is a huge statue of Father Thames. It is now an upmarket hotel while the PLA resides in the less glamorous environs of Gravesend.

Walk left, crossing the busy road and head down towards the Tower. All tourist eyes will be looking into the Tower to the left. We will keep our eyes to the right since just past the ticket offices for the Tower, there is a much smaller tower with a long and fascinating history (it often has an ice-cream van parked just in front of it).

Stop 2

This little tower, labelled the London Hydraulic Power Company, is the entrance to a subway under the river built in the 1860s, well before Tower Bridge. While the river was a great means of transport it was also a major barrier for anyone trying to cross it. The only way of getting across was either walking to London Bridge or by boat. Any ordinary bridge would, of course, strangle the great warehouses upstream. An enterprising Victorian, James Greathead, decided that if you can't go over it, you'll have to go under it. Accordingly, a tunnel was built seven metres under the Thames to carry a railway from one bank to the other. A single carriage for 12 passengers was pulled back and forth by steam engines. The enterprise was a disaster, the hauling mechanism kept breaking down, and it closed after a few months. It was then converted to a foot tunnel and every day 20,000 people paid 1/2d to walk under the river.

The opening of Tower Bridge put an end to the profitability of the tunnel and it was converted to carrying water under high pressure which provided power to drive lifts, cranes and fire hydrants. Customers included the Palladium and Coliseum which used water power to open safety curtains and drive revolving stages. The system only closed in 1977 but the tunnel is still in use and now carries telecommunications cables.

Walk to the river bank by the Tower.

Stop 3

You are now standing by the Pool of London, the City's historic port. Upstream you see London Bridge close to the site of the original Roman Bridge. On the north bank you should be able to spy Billingsgate, identified by the fish on its weather vane. Next to it you can glimpse Custom House where importers paid their tolls. This short stretch of river was the site of the Legal Quays set up by Elizabeth I which lasted for 250 years. On the south bank behind HMS Belfast, you can see the enormous structure of Hay's Wharf dating from the 1850s. At its height 80% of the dry goods such as tea that was imported into London came through this wharf.

Walk along the riverbank, go under Tower Bridge and then back onto the riverside.

Stop 4

You're now standing on what used to be Irongate Wharf. For many years it specialised in grain imports but by the end of the nineteenth century many of the Jewish migrants fleeing from the anti-Semitism of the Russian empire disembarked here. They then had an even more perilous journey to reach the safety of the Jewish community of Whitechapel confronted on all sides by unscrupulous middlemen, con artists and worse.

Walk past the massive and hideous Tower Hotel, regularly voted one of the ugliest buildings in London. We arrive at St Katharine Docks. Cross over the locks to stand outside the Dock Managers' House.

Stop 5

St Katharine Docks are the first of the enclosed docks that we come across on this walk. They were built on the site of a medieval monastery and hospital which by the 1800s was an overcrowded slum. The building of the dock destroyed over 1000 houses and made 11,000 people homeless. The landlords were compensated, the tenants were not. They were forced to leave to add to the overcrowding elsewhere in the East End.

Built in 1828 by the famous engineer, Thomas Telford, the docks were revolutionary in that goods could be winched straight from the boats' holds into the warehouses above. However, they were not particularly successful, being too small to accommodate the growing size of ships. They tended to specialise in high value goods such as ivory and spices. This was because the docks were closest to central London markets making the vulnerable road journeys much shorter. There were also detachments of soldiers nearby, based in the Tower and the Royal Mint just to the north of the docks, who could protect the most valuable goods.

Walk round to your right with the dock on your left to go down Marble Quay and bear right down St Katharine's Way and stop by Alderman Stairs.

Stop 6

The buildings in front of you such as Millers Wharf are examples of classic Docklands architecture. These great warehouses lined the Thames from the Tower to the Isle of Dogs with their distinctive wide windows and balconies and with their winches above to shift the goods down to the street.. The only access to the river bank was the stairs which often date back to medieval times and punctuated the warehouses every few hundred metres. At the bottom of the stairs would be the boats to take passengers up and down the river.

A few metres further on take the signposted passage to the Thames Path.

Stop 7

A glorious view is in front of you stretching from Bermondsey to London Bridge and beyond. Opposite is Butlers Wharf, now home to up market restaurants but previously it was a major food importer including reputedly the largest tea warehouse in the world. To its left, is the outlet of one of the lost rivers of London, the Neckinger. It formed the boundary with Jacob's Island, a notorious slum which was described as the 'very capital of cholera' in 1849.

It was here that Dickens set the climactic scene of his most famous novel, Oliver Twist. Bill Sykes, having killed Nancy, is surrounded by a mob on the island. He attempts to swing over the creek but inadvertently hangs himself leaving Fagin to be captured and taken to Newgate.

Walk along the embankment and you are soon diverted along a passage to rejoin the road. The inlet you walk past is the western entrance to the London Docks built from 1801 onwards. Walk twenty metres along the road to your right and in front of you are the great gates of the docks.

Stop 8

You are standing at the western end of the London Docks and you're looking at the basin where the ships would wait until the tide was high to sail back out onto the river. The gates and walls are reminiscent of those of a prison and indeed their role was to keep undesirables out and goods in. It was in front of these gates that the Call On took place in the mornings and afternoons where hundreds of men would line up hoping for a few hours work.

Follow the path between the basin and the wall then drop down the stairs to the left.

Stop 9

You are standing at the south western edge of the western basin of the London Docks. The dimensions were enormous. You can see the length of the basin stretching away in front of you. The width was almost as great but has now been filled in by new housing. Its depth was around 8 metres and this vast amount of earth was shifted by hand by teams of mainly Irish 'Navvies'. The word comes from 'Navigators' because men like these had built the navigations, or canals, and went on to build the railways.

Walk along the side of the dock next to the water's edge. After 200 metres or so, you are forced to turn left. On your right is where the central entrance to the London Docks entered the Western Basin. The true dimensions of the basin can be seen from this point. Keep walking along the side of the channel; after another few hundred metres, you bear right to enter Tobacco Dock with its ships safely in dry dock.

Stop 10

As its name suggests these were very secure warehouses, holding precious imports. Chief amongst them was obviously tobacco, but there is another clue over the main gates. Barrels and hogs heads are displayed showing that these were also warehouses for imported alcohol. Tobacco Dock demonstrates that not all the regeneration of the Docklands was successful. During the early years it was launched as an upmarket shopping centre but that has long since failed and now it is an events and marketing venue.

Walk up the stairs and turn left along Wapping Lane following the line of the warehouses and take the first left into Pennington Street. Here you can glimpse what the warehouses used to look like. Just inside the gates and to your right you may glimpse a statue of a small boy and an enormous tiger. This commemorates a celebrated incident in 1857 when a tiger escaped from Charles Jamrach's Animal Emporium and picked up an eight year old boy who foolishly was trying to pet the runaway beast. Heroically Jamrach forced the tiger to let go of his prey but was still sued by the boy's parents. The tale is recounted in 'Jamrach's Menagerie' by Carol Birch which was short-listed for the Booker Prize in 2011.

Turn right up Chigwell Hill and then with great care cross The Highway and walk up Cannon Street Road. The Ratcliffe Highway is an old Roman road running along the banks of the Thames and in the early nineteenth century had an evil reputation. In 1811, in the space of 12 days two attacks on the occupants of two different houses led to the murders of seven people. The suspect committed suicide and was buried with a stake through his heart at the top of Cannon Street Road. Thomas de Quincy, he of 'Confessions of an Opium Eater', wrote an essay entitled 'On murder, Considered as one of the Fine Arts' on the case.

Walk up Cannon Street Road to the entrance to the church of St George's in the East.

Stop 11

This church was one of Queen Anne's 50 churches to bring Protestantism to the rapidly growing city. In the end only eleven were built, six of them, including St George's, by Nicholas Hawksmoor. Badly damaged in the Blitz a modern church nestles within the original shell.

Walk round the church into the graveyard where there is a handsome tomb to the Raine family; brewers and well-known philanthropists of the eighteenth century.

With your back to the church bear left towards Cable Street where you will see a great mural on the wall of the old Town Hall.

Stop 12

The mural commemorates the Battle of Cable Street on 4 October 1936. Oswald Mosley, leader of the British Union of Fascists (BUF), was attempting to lead a march through the Jewish community of Whitechapel. Blocked by a massive protest at Aldgate, the police tried to force a route for the fascists into the East End along Cable Street. Three sets of barricades including an overturned lorry stopped the police from breaking through and eventually Mosley dispersed his members westwards.

Cable Street marked the tipping point for pre-war fascism in Britain. While marches and attacks on Jewish premises continued the momentum of the BUF had been broken. The Public Order Act was passed in 1937 which banned the wearing of political uniforms and controlled demonstrations.

The mural vividly illustrates the events of 1936, with police horses, truncheons, chamberpots, overturned lorries and includes a fascist with a marked resemblance to Hitler dressed only in his underwear!

Retrace your steps straight across the graveyard, noting the sad and derelict remains of a nature study centre set up for the children of the slums between the wars, to cross the Highway and walk down Wapping Lane. Follow the Lane past Tobacco Dock until on your left you reach Raine Street named after the benefactor whose grave we saw.

Stop 13

Just down the street there is a charity school founded by Raine's in 1719. The stern injunction to its pupils can still be read over the entrance: 'Come in and Learn your Duty to God and Man'.

Retrace your steps and continue to walk down Wapping Lane. Shortly you come to the church of St Peter's London Docks.

Stop 14

This an extraordinary place, a fine example of high Victorian gothic. It was built in 1866 as part of the first Anglican mission to the poor of London. While it is a part of the Church of England it is very much in the Catholic tradition and this is exemplified in the decoration and atmosphere of the church.

Continue down Wapping Lane and shortly cross the road and walk across Wapping Green to a pub on its far corner.

Stop 15

This is Turner's Old Star, named after JMW Turner. The famous painter brought his mistress, Sophia Booth, from Margate to London and installed her as the landlady of the Old Star pub. He adopted her surname and was known in the area as Puggy Booth. Here he created some of his most famous paintings including The Fighting Temeraire, painted just over the river at Bermondsey.

There is another, more chilling plaque on the pub. In the lane by the side of the pub a woman, Lydia Rogers, was found guilty of witchcraft in 1658. This was not a unique event in Wapping, there had been other instances of women being accused of witchcraft. In 1652, Joan Peterson was hanged at Tyburn for supposedly bewitching a wealthy elderly woman.

Walk down the Tench Street and then turn into the green and walk through to Green Bank. This was named after the original embankment to drain the marsh at Wapping by Dutch engineers in the sixteenth century.

Cross Scandrett Street and walk into the graveyard opposite St John's Parish Church.

Stop 16

The church was built in 1756 but badly damaged in the Blitz and only the central steeple survives. Next to the church is its fine charity school with the children dressed in blue (blue coats signify a charity school). In the churchyard itself there is a plaque to one of the heroes of the Civil War, Thomas Rainsborough, who ended up as commander of Cromwell's navy and the spokesman for the Levellers, the more democratic and radical wing of the parliamentary forces. His funeral in Wapping was attended by thousands of his supporters.

These are all signs that Wapping in the seventeenth and eighteenth century was a relatively prosperous village. It was only when it was effectively sealed off from the outside world by the building of the docks that its slide into deepest poverty began.

Walk through the graveyard to Wapping High Street, turn right and within a few metres you arrive at Pier Head.

Stop 17

This was the central entrance into the London Docks, the course of the channel is still clearly recognisable. The beautiful houses overlooking the river once belonged to the dock managers and custom officials. Today, Graham Norton lives in one of the finest.

Walk back along Wapping High Street where you pass a tiny pub, the Town of Ramsgate.

Stop 18

This is one of the oldest and most historic pubs on the river and claims to have first existed in the 1460s. Previously called the Red Cow, supposedly after an infamous bar maid, it took its current name from the Ramsgate boats that unloaded their fish at the Stairs next to the pub. You can get down to the river at low tide by using Wapping Old Stairs. This is a very atmospheric place; it is possible that this is the site of Execution Dock where hundreds of 'pirates' met their end. The pub claims that a post only visible at low tide is where their bodies were tied so that the river would cover them three times. Legend has it that Captain Bligh of Mutiny on the Bounty fame met Fletcher Christian here. What is definitely true is that Judge Jeffreys, the Hanging Judge, was captured in the pub in 1688, disguised as a woman, as he attempted to flee England after the fall of his master James II. Jeffreys was taken to the Tower where he died from liver disease soon after.

Continue walking east along the High Street.

In front of you is some more classic Docklands architecture; two gangways linking the riverside wharfs with the warehouses behind. These are now used as summer balconies for the flat dwellers but they were built as an essential part of the Docks economy. Goods could be wheel-barrowed between the two buildings rather than having them winched down into the street and then winched up into the opposite building.

Soon you pass the boatyard for the Thames River Police, Waterside Gardens with great views of the river and Rotherhithe and Wapping New Stairs, another possible site of Execution Dock. Next comes the Captain Kidd, another lovely riverside pub housed in a nineteenth century warehouse with beautiful Thames views.

The warehouses rise up on either side. You pass King Henry's Wharf and Gun Wharf commemorating Henry VIII establishing the foundries to make the cannons for his Navy here.

Finally you arrive at Wapping Station. This could be the end of your walk as frequent trains take you south to Canada Water and the Jubilee Line or north to Whitechapel on the District and Metropolitan lines. Alternatively you can continue onto Part 2 of the walk.

Stop 19

Whether continuing or not, the station is a site of historic importance as it is still using the original shaft which leads down to the first tunnel ever built under a navigable river. Built between 1825 and 1843, it is the masterpiece of Sir Marc Brunel, father of Isambard Brunel. The latter worked on it and nearly died in it. The actual tunnel is a remarkable achievement; its techniques and innovations made possible the development of mass urban transportation. After all, most great cities are built on rivers and the ability to get beneath them is crucial to the development of a modern transport system. While the station has some notice boards about its history, the full story can be seen in the Brunel Museum at Rotherhithe just over the river. Even more exciting is the Mayflower Pub, a gorgeous and historic pub standing on the site from which the ship carrying the Pilgrim Fathers set off for Massachusetts in 1620.

Walking London's Docklands – from Wapping to Canary Wharf

We start the second part of our walk from Wapping Station. Turn right out of the station and walk eastwards down the high street. After a few hundred metres you bear left briefly into Garnet Street which apparently gave Johnny Speight the name for Alf, the patriarch of 'Till Death Us Do Part'.

Immediately turn right up Wapping Wall. *Details of what you'll see on this walk start on the page which follows this map...*

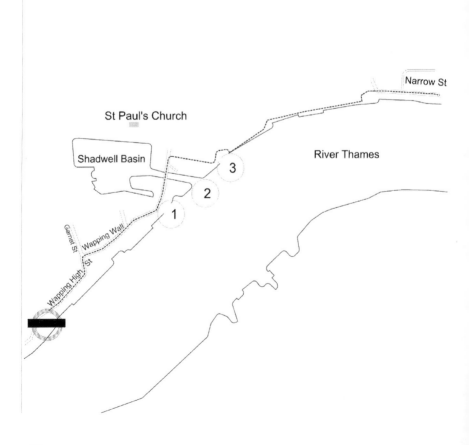

1 Prospect of Whitby

2 Eastern Dock Basin

3 Rotherhithe Road Tunnel Rotunda

4 Limehouse Basin

5 Regent's Canal

6 St Anne's Church and 'The Wisdom of Solomon'

7 The Grapes

8 Limekiln Dock

9 Guard House, Memorial Plaque and Dock Master House

10 Museum of Docklands

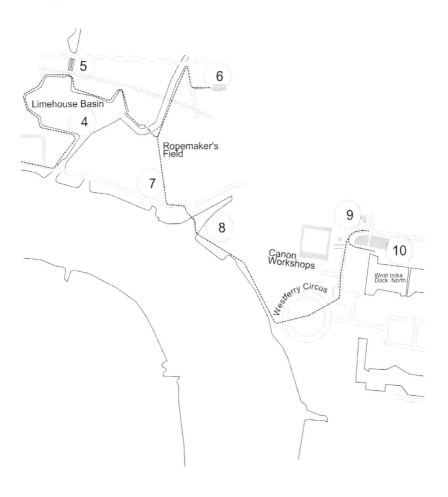

Stop 1

You soon come to another historic pub, the Prospect of Whitby, named after a coal carrying barge from the north east. It claims to be the oldest extant pub on the river being built in 1520. Both JMW Turner and the American Artist James Whistler sketched the river view while Charles Dickens and Samuel Pepys drank here. It was also where the first fuchsia arrived in Britain. It's got a great courtyard with a wonderful view entered through a small gate just to the left of the pub.

Opposite the pub you see the tower of the Wapping Hydraulic Power Company. This was one of the pumping stations providing the power which once went under the Thames at the little tower we noticed at the very start of the first part of the walk.

Stop 2

As you turn the corner by the Prospect of Whitby, you come to the great eastern basin of the London Docks. This was built in the 1850s to expand the London Docks and make them accessible to the ever larger vessels being used. This was only a stopgap solution. By the beginning of the 20th Century, many ships were too large to enter the London Docks and had to be unloaded elsewhere with goods being ferried down to the warehouses of Wapping. These ships could use the Royal Victoria and Albert Docks five miles downstream.

Walk across the bridge and note the elegant spire of St Paul's Church across the dock. It is called the Church of the Sea Captains as 75 are buried inside. Captain Cook worshipped there and his eldest son was baptised in the church as was Jane Randolph, mother of Thomas Jefferson, the third president of the United States. The church was rebuilt in the early 1800s.

A few dozen metres beyond the bridge a small passage on your right leads to the King Edward VII Memorial Park. This was built as part of a slum clearance programme on the site of the Shadwell Fish Market.

Stop 3

The rotunda you pass is the air vent for the Rotherhithe Road Tunnel, you can still see the London County Council insignia in the iron work. On its northern side you can see a memorial to some of the great explorers who set off from near this point in the sixteenth and seventeenth centuries to discover the North West passage across Canada. They never made it and some died in the attempt. Today, with global warming the route is open during the late summer months.

Continue along the Thames Path, past the sprawling and ugly Free Trade Wharf housing development. You will soon notice some beautiful late eighteenth century warehouses built by the East India Company. These are all that remain of much more extensive wharves many of which were burnt in a devastating fire in the mid nineteenth century. Notice also the tracks and old wagons which were used to transport goods within the complex.

The path briefly deviates away from the Thames and shortly takes you onto Narrow Street as you continue your way eastwards.

Narrow Street is built on the original dyke that drained the Wapping marshes in the sixteenth century. It's narrow now but used to be much narrower. A report in 1865 noted that it was never wider than 8 metres.

Rejoin the Thames Path for more beautiful views in both directions. Soon you reach the Narrows, the old dockmaster's house, now a 'gastropub' owned by Gordon Ramsay. Walk up the stairs, cross the road, turn left and then right into the great marina.

Stop 4

Now the home of narrow boats and luxury yachts, the Limehouse Basin was once one of the great trading centres of London. Built in 1820, the basin linked the docks to England's canal system via the Regents Canal. Goods from around the world would be unloaded in the docks and transported by river into the Basin, loaded on narrow boats and then taken round London and up to the midlands and the north. Manufactured goods travelled in the opposite direction; from the industrial heartlands for export overseas.

The basin is also the end point of the Limehouse Cut which links the Thames to the River Lea. This was built in the 1760s so the industries built along the banks of the Lea could easily access the markets of London.

Walk around the basin to the far side where the Regents Canal enters the Basin.

Stop 5

In front of you are the locks which mark the end of the Regents Canal; the canal runs for 14 kilometres around north London to Paddington where it joins with the Grand Union Canal. Notice also the railway viaduct which shares the scene. This is one of the earliest railways in the world, built in 1840 to provide a secure link between the East and West India Docks and the markets of the City of London.

The lines are still used by the Docklands Light Railway, ferrying people between the old and new financial centres of London: the City and Canary Wharf.

Carry on walking around the Basin and cross over the second canal, the Limehouse Cut. This is the oldest London canal as it opened in 1769 to ease the journey for the grain coming down the River Lea into London. The canal meant that goods no longer had to wait on the right tides to use the Lea and cut out the journey around the Isle of Dogs. Walk along the side of the Cut, going under the railway viaduct until some stairs appear on the right. Go up these stairs, cross Newell Street, admiring the fine early Georgian houses and in front of you is one of the greatest churches of the East End, St. Anne's Limehouse.

Stop 6

This is another Hawksmoor church built in 1730. St. Anne's is archetypal Hawksmoor: a very solid, powerful building approached through a narrow passage, the aim of which is to overwhelm the visitor.

The church has always been linked to the sea. At the top of the Tower, flies the White Ensign of the Royal Navy since Queen Anne decreed that the new church would be the place for captains to register important events that happened at sea. Alongside it is a golden ball which became a Trinity House navigation mark to aid traffic on the Thames. The clock is the highest in a London church and was the first to be illuminated at night. The reason for this was that St. Anne's was the crucial link between Greenwich Observatory which set accurate time and the Pool of London who needed to set their chronometers accurately.

In the churchyard there is an extraordinary monument; a four sided pyramid bearing the inscription 'The Wisdom of Solomon' in English and Hebrew. No-one knows quite why it is there or what its original purpose might have been although recently some novelists have suggested Hawksmoor was interested in the occult and this may have some link to those enthusiasms.

Retrace your steps back along the canal and then cut across Ropemakers' Park back to Narrow Street.

Stop 7

On your right you should see the Grapes, one of the most famous pubs on the Thames which dates back to 1583. Both Pepys and Dickens used the pub regularly while Turner and Whistler painted the

Thames near here. Its current owner is Sir Ian McKellen and behind the bar you can see Gandalf's staff as used in the Lord of the Rings trilogy. Alongside the Grapes is a row of beautiful houses dating back to the seventeenth and eighteenth century. Francis Bacon lived in number 80 while David Lean, the film director, also lived here.

Before we leave Limehouse it is worth remembering that at the turn of the twentieth century the area was famed as the centre of the Chinese community in London. Many were sailors abandoned by their shipping companies. Writers such as Oscar Wilde, Conan Doyle and especially Sax Rohmer who wrote the Fu Manchu novels made the area notorious for its opium dens and 'white slavery' as prostitution was sometimes known. There are now very few signs of that once thriving community as in the 1960s it relocated to Soho.

Continue walking down Narrow Street until another sign directs you back onto the Thames Path.

Stop 8

As you cross Limekiln Dock, halfway up on the left you will see the ghostly remains of 'J & R Wilson Ship Stores' and some very old warehouses. With a little imagination it's possible to visualise what this must have looked like in its hey-day 150 years ago. Limekiln Dock and indeed Limehouse is named after the chalk that was heated to create lime for the building industry in the middle ages. The Dock itself is the mouth of one of the hidden rivers of London, the Black Ditch which flowed from Shoreditch through Stepney before reaching the Thames.

Continue walking on the Thames Path with the office blocks of Canary Wharf in front of you.

You're now on the Isle of Dogs. It's not an Island, in fact it is a great peninsula jutting out into the Thames and until 1800 was almost uninhabited marshland. No-one knows quite how it got its name which first appeared in the sixteenth century. It may be a corruption of the 'dykes' that were built to drain the marshes or perhaps it's from the dogs that Henry VIII kennelled here.

The area was completely transformed in the space of a few years when, in 1800, Robert Milligan gained permission to build the great West India Docks. He was a sugar trader and slave owner based in the West Indies and was horrified at the pillaging and delays of his cargoes. He successfully petitioned Parliament for permission to build an enclosed Dock for the West Indies trade. Eventually four great docks were cut across the Isle. Ships would enter from the east, be unloaded in the import docks and then turn round to be reloaded in the export docks. Critically, the docks were surrounded by a six metre high wall and lined with five story warehouses. The West India Docks could handle 600 ships at a time with much greater security and safety than before.

Walk across Westferry Circus and bear right into Columbus Court-yard. Walk down the steps on your right, bear left and then right into Hertsmere Road. (There is so much building work going on that any directions around this area may well change.) As you walk up Herts-mere Road on your left you will see a small, circular hut which used to be for the armed guards who patrolled the area.

Stop 9

On your right you will soon come to a great memorial plaque detailing the great and good including the Prime Minister, William Pitt, who came together to build the dock in order to 'offer complete security and ample accommodation (hitherto not afforded) to the shipping and produce of the West Indies at this wealthy port'.

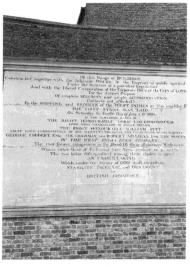

As we've seen not everyone shared in the wealth the port generated. The docks had been built by hand, often by Irish migrants and many of them stayed on to become dock workers. They formed the poorest and most insecure part of London's workforce.

Walk a few metres further on and you see the fine Dock Masters House and then the great Dock Gates where the Call-On took place.

Retrace your steps and enter the docks passing the original ware-houses and offices to reach the entrance of the wonderful Museum of Docklands.

Stop 10

The Museum explores the history of the docks from Roman times through to its regeneration in the last forty years. The museum is a fitting end to the walk as it puts so much of what you have seen on the walk into context.

Finally

The area around Canary Wharf is full of places to eat and drink including a café in the Museum of Docklands. Nearest stations are Westferry or West India Quay on the Docklands Light Railway or Canary Wharf on the Jubilee line.

If you still have a bit of energy left, there are many other places you could visit on or near the Isle of Dogs. In front of you there is Canary Wharf, the centre of the regeneration of the Docklands with shopping malls, entertainment and office blocks. Further south, there is Mudchute Park, named after all the mud that was excavated from the Docks and then 'shot' to form raised ground in the middle of the marsh. It is now home to a City Farm and the remains of the anti-aircraft gun emplacements built in the Second World War to protect the docks. Nearest DLR station is Mudchute. To the east of the museum is Cold-harbour; a row of stately Georgian houses including the Gun pub which claims Lord Nelson as a customer who came here for secret liaisons with Lady Hamilton in an upstairs boudoir. Further on there are the remains of the East India Docks at Blackwall of which only the basin remains and is now a nature reserve. Finally there are the delights of Trinity Buoy Wharf, an extraordinary place where the River Lea meets the Thames. It's where West Ham United were formed as the factory team of Thames Iron Works and is the site of London's only light house which is now home to the Longplayer, a millennium project where non-repetitive music will be played for the next thousand years. Nearest DLR station East India.

Regency London

The Regency, if we were to strictly define it, lasted only from 1811 to 1820 when the future George IV ruled for his ailing father who had suffered periodic bouts of insanity. Many historians, however, use the term to describe a much longer period from around 1790 to the accession of Victoria in 1837 and we are going to follow that usage. This fifty year period was marked by massive change in Britain. It saw victory in the wars against Napoleonic France, Britain's domination of the seas, the rapid growth of the British Empire and expansion of maritime trade, the development of industry and manufacturing as the Industrial Revolution took root across Britain and a revolution in transport, with firstly the development of the canal system and then the introduction of the railways. Culturally, it was the age of Jane Austen, Wordsworth, Keats and Shelley as well as the dandyism, amorality and profligacy of Beau Brummel and the Regent himself. It was also a time of controversy, debate and repression. The American War of Independence and the French Revolution raised searching questions about power, democracy and human rights. Some thinkers began to challenge the deeply unequal world that they saw around them. These included radicals like Tom Paine, author of the Rights of Man and Mary Wollstonecraft who wrote 'Vindication of the Rights of Women' and has been described as the first English feminist.

London was at the heart of all these economic and cultural changes and in the process transformed itself yet again.

London was growing rapidly at the turn of the nineteenth century, its population expanding along with its economy. Already it was the pre-eminent city in Europe with a population of around a million. It was a city based on trade. The new enclosed docks in the east were channelling wealth into the city from the growing British Empire. Fortunes were being made from trade with India, China, the West Indies and Africa. But London was also at the heart of the boom in manufacturing industry. While radical new techniques were being developed in the mills of Lancashire and Yorkshire, London remained the greatest manufacturing city in the world throughout much of the nineteenth century. During the Regency period it was the centre for the production of food, furniture, clothes, ships as well as luxury goods. Even by 1851 when the northern manufacturing centres were booming, London had 370,000 manufacturing workers, more than the entire population of Manchester. They were concentrated in industries on the outskirts of the city such as the riverside villages of Wapping and Limehouse, Spitalfields and Whitechapel in the east and around the Regent's Canal which linked the docks with the industrial heartlands of the midlands and the north.

At the end of the period a new form of transport, the railways, came to compete with the canals and revolutionised Britain's economy. Great termini were built round the edge of London; Paddington, Euston, Kings Cross, Liverpool Street, Waterloo and London Bridge. Not only did this lead to the massive geographical expansion of London, it also aided trade to move in and out of London more quickly, cheaply and efficiently. This wealth was being used to transform London. The profligate Prince Regent was working with his favourite architect, John Nash, who he'd already used to build the Brighton Pavilion, to launch London's first significant piece of town planning. This was a 'Via Triumphalis' which was to link a new park in the north west corner of central London to the Regent's London home overlooking the Mall and his new residence at Buckingham Palace. So Regent's Park and Regent's Street were born, the latter conveniently separating artisan Soho from wealthy Mayfair.

John Nash was one of a remarkable triumvirate of developers and architects at the turn of the nineteenth century. The other two were father and son, James and Decimus Burton. Despite or perhaps because of being the tenth son, Decimus's work was spectacular and his father was a genius at smoothing out the obstacles en route.

What was to become Regent's Park was in 1810 market gardens supplying London. With the patronage of the Prince Regent, the Burtons began buying up the land. The plan was to build grand terraces around the perimeter of the park with fifty six villas for the very wealthy. The buildings were spectacular, often based on classical, Greek designs they were much more flamboyant than the Georgian style they replaced. Heavy use was made of stucco; decorative plaster on the outside of the houses while all sorts of influences were at play to beautify the houses. Nash made reference to Moorish designs in some of his work while Burton looked to the classical statues of Ancient Greece whilst using modern production techniques to create them.

As the housing in Regent's Park was being developed so were some of its other facilities. The Zoological Society London opened the Zoo in 1828 within the Park transferring animals from the Tower of London. A boating lake fed by the river Tyburn was built at the centre; it had to be closed and made shallower after 40 people drowned when ice on the frozen lake collapsed in January 1867. Nash integrated the proposed Regent's Canal into the scheme but opposition from some of the wealthy stakeholders forced it round the periphery of the park. After all, at the beginning of the nineteenth century canals were the key transport link for the economy, the motorways of their time. It was much, much later that they became an asset in inflating property prices.

Regent's Park has always retained its cachet as a fashionable address. Other parts of Regency London were not so lucky. The area round the Canal flourished in the nineteenth century as one of the hubs of manufacturing industry but as London lost its manufacturing base after the war it entered a steady decline. It became an area notorious for its on-street drug dealing, rough sleeping and prostitution. It's only in the last twenty or thirty years that the area round Kings Cross has been transformed in an enormous regeneration project which has attracted The Guardian, Facebook and Google amongst many others.

Today, the area is still full of contrasts: grand houses, peaceful canals and sculptured parks rub shoulders with tourist attractions like Camden Lock, social housing, dilapidated factories, gleaming tech headquarters and ancient, forgotten churches.

Walking Regency London – along the Regent's canal

In this walk we are going to explore the two sides of Regency London. We start with the opulence and luxury of the new West End that was transformed by the Prince Regent's grandiose schemes for London. But we end deep in the industrial heartland of London where the wealth was created which funded the life-style of the rich.

This walk starts at Baker Street Station and finishes at Kings Cross Station.

Details of what you'll see on this walk start on the page which follows this map...

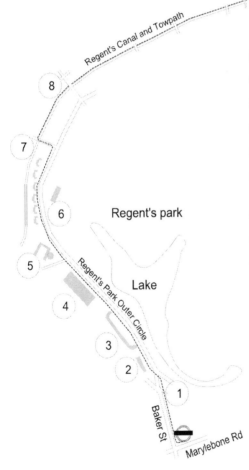

1 Regent's Park

2 Clarence Terrace

3 Sussex Place

4 Hanover Terrace

5 Regent's Park Mosque

6 Hanover Lodge and Winfield House

7 Regent's Canal

8 Macclesfield Bridge

9 Floating Restaurant

10 Gilbey's Gin and Railway Interchange

Come out of the station onto Marylebone Road, turn right and right again to walk north up Baker Street passing the Sherlock Holmes' museum at 221B Baker Street and crossing Park Road until you reach the entrance to Regents Park at Clarence Terrace.

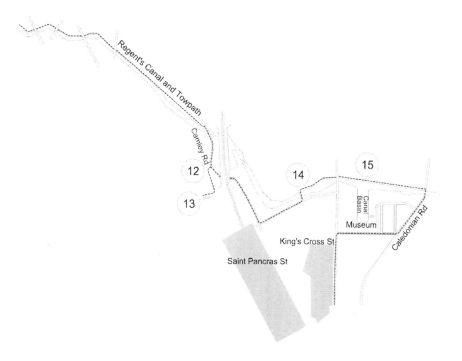

11 Camden Market and Ice Wharf

12 St Pancras Graveyard

13 St Pancras Old Church

14 Lock and Coal Drops Yard

15 Battlebridge Basin

Stop 1

Regents Park in the late eighteenth century was farmland, supplying London with fresh food. Over twenty years it was transformed into one of the most desirable addresses in London by the efforts of John Nash and James and Decimus Burton who built grand terraces and desirable villas around the periphery of the park.

Stop 2

We are now outside Clarence Terrace. This is the smallest of the eight terraces in the park but a worthy introduction to its glories. It is rigorously classical in design using Greek inspired columns to create an imposing entrance. Designed by Decimus Burton, it was built by his father, James. There is no reason why you should not walk along the road in front of the terraces. They are open to the public.

Continue walking along the Outer Circle and you soon come to the next great building.

Stop 3

This is Sussex Place, now the London Business School. This was designed by John Nash in a distinctive 'Neo-Moorish' style. It has obvious links with the much more flamboyant Brighton Pavilion which Nash also designed.

Stop 4

Next is Hanover Terrace, the most spectacular building on the western side of the park. This was also designed by Nash and is adorned with Greek-inspired statues of the goddesses. The building uses the famous Wedgewood Blue design so popular in the Regency period. This is our first reference to the burgeoning production of the industrial revolution which was transforming British society at the beginning of the nineteenth century. As you walk past the beautifully designed entrances with their blue plaques detailing past occupants you're in fact on a raised road. The buildings were built quickly and relatively cheaply as the soil that was dug for the foundations was just piled in front of the houses. The basements with their restricted views and proneness to damp were used to house the servants.

As you walk along, keep an eye out for the lamp posts. They all look identical but closer examination shows that some were installed in the reign of George IV, others in the reign of William IV with the majority modern replacements bearing Elizabeth's name - EIIR.

Our next Stop is also modern, the great Regents Park Mosque.

Stop 5

This was originally proposed by Lord Lloyd of Dolobran, a Quaker and diplomat, as a tribute to the loyalty of Muslims to the Empire during the Second World War. Whilst the site was reserved during the war it took until 1977 before the great mosque finally opened. Today 5,000 worshippers can gather to pray in its great hall.

Stop 6

Our next stop is Hanover Lodge, one of the fifty six villas planned for the park. Of the fifty six only nine were built and today only six survive. One of those that was rebuilt in the 1930s is Winfield House on your right. You're unlikely to glimpse the house as it is hidden behind an imposing hedge. You'll probably see the Stars and Stripes, however, as this is the residence of the US Ambassador to the UK. It was rebuilt by Barbara Hutton, the Woolworth's heiress

which she later sold to the US government for $1.

As you follow the road round you pass six more villas which at first glance may be thought to be part of the original layout of the park. In fact they are modern, built between 1988 and 2004, by Prince Charles' favourite architect, Quinlan Terry. They are supposed to represent different neoclassical architectural styles such Gothick, Ionic and Regency.

When you reach the end of the villas take the footpath on the left over the bridge to cross the Regent's Canal. Turn right by the side of the bridge and right again to find yourself on the towpath by the bridge.

Stop 7

The Regent's Canal came at the end of the great era of canal building that transformed England at the end of the eighteenth century. The canals had reached London at Paddington by 1801 which enabled goods and raw materials to access the capital from the Midlands and North. But that didn't help transporting goods for export as Paddington was a long way from the Thames and especially the great Docks that were being built in the east. The Regent's Canal was seen as the missing piece in the jigsaw linking the industrial revolution of the north with the imperial markets overseas.

To begin with, the Canal struggled for finance until the project was taken up by John Nash as part of his grand plans and in the eight years to 1820, the canal was completed. It was a major feat of engineering, following as far as possible the contours round the centre of London.

One of the logistical challenges is right in front of you. The bridge used to carry within its structure the hidden River Tyburn. This rises on Hampstead Heath and once fed Regent's Park lake, passing Marble Arch where it gave its name to the Tyburn Tree, the traditional site of execution, before flowing into the Thames at Pimlico.

Start walking eastwards, away from the bridge. In a few hundred metres, another bridge cuts the canal.

Stop 8

Look up at the great black columns supporting the bridge and note that they come from Coalbrookdale, one of the great centres of the industrial revolution in England. It was here that Abraham Darby pioneered the world's first coke fired blast furnace producing high quality cast iron. Nothing demonstrates better the link between the burgeoning power of British manufacturing and the transformation of transport than these

columns, made in Shropshire and then floated down the canals to build the bridges over those same canals.

Look again at the outside of the columns and you'll notice some strange horizontal grooves on their sides. These were made by the tow ropes by which horses pulled the barges along the canals. The problem is that if the grooves were on the outside of the columns the horses would be garrotted! The columns have, in fact, been moved. In 1874 the bridge was all but destroyed by an enormous explosion when a barge carrying gunpowder exploded. When the bridge was rebuilt, the columns were changed around to even up the erosion from the ropes.

Continue to walk down the canal. You are now walking through London Zoo with the aviary on your left and some of the enclosures for animals across the canal. Keep your eyes peeled and you could see warthogs or African wild dogs.

Many of the bridges carry their makers' mark which testify to a very different capital city, one in which manufacturing was integral to its economy. One of the bridges, for instance, was made by Manor Iron Works of Chelsea and another smelted in Oxford Street.

You come soon to an abrupt bend in the canal with a short basin in front of you.

Stop 9

In front of you, somewhat incongruously, is a bright red Chinese junk, the canal's only floating restaurant. It's moored in the Cumberland Basin, this used to be a spur off the main canal which supplied a market further into London.

Keep walking down the canal and you will soon notice that its nature has changed. While there are still a few grand houses the environment is now more built up and more industrialised. There are still a few quirks along the way like the ornamental cow decorating someone's canal side terrace.

You soon come to two crenelated buildings on either side of the canal. On your right is the Pirate Castle, a youth club offering canoeing and other activities to local young people. On the left is a pumping station which pumps water in to cool the electricity cables that run beneath your feet. Indeed the reason why the towpath is in such good repair is partly because it serves as the route for high tension electricity cables round north London.

Just beyond the castles there is a large white building on your right; this is the old factory for Gilbey's Gin, a quintessential London drink. As you walk down the towpath, it suddenly rises up and turns into a bridge by the side of a huge warehouse.

Stop 10

This historic building is in many ways a symbol of the changes sweeping London in the nineteenth century. It served as an interchange between the canal system and the new revolutionary mode of transport: the railways. The heyday of the canals lasted only around fifty years before the railways offered a faster and more reliable means of transport. This warehouse used to be linked to rail tracks coming down from the north bringing coal and other raw materials to the city. Barges would be moored underneath the building in bays which can still be glimpsed, to transport goods round London.

In a hundred metres you come to Camden Lock, one of the top tourist attractions in London. It started in the 1970s to replace the manufacturing industry which was in terminal decline and has been an enormous success. On summer weekends this area can be full to bursting and probably best avoided. Throughout the year, there is a steady stream of visitors and it is a good place to grab some street food from the stalls originating from countries around the world.

Stop 11

We cross the bridge over the canal to a Wetherspoon's pub, The Ice Wharf. Its name reminds us that this was a major warehouse for ice harvested from the lakes of Norway in the winter, transported by canal and then stored in deep underground shafts for use during the summer. Outside the pub is a statue representing the workers in that perilous industry.

The small building just beyond it is the lock keeper's cottage which houses an exhibition telling the story of the canal. The locks at Camden are the first for 20 miles as you come from the west which demonstrates just how accurate was the construction of the canal as it hugged the contours around London.

Cross back over the canal at the road bridge and continue eastwards along the towpath.

The canal zigzags under half a dozen road bridges, hitting each at a 90 degree angle, thus cutting down on construction costs. On many of the bridges you will see the indentations caused by the tow ropes as they cut into the bricks or the iron bars used to protect the bridges. Another piece of canal architecture to look out for are small cuttings into the side of the canal, measuring around 10 metres by 1 metre. These are for rescuing horses who may have stumbled or been pulled into the canal by the barges. While the canal's depth is only about 1.5 metres, horses couldn't clamber out so these indentations have ramps leading out of the water so the horses could be led back onto dry land.

The canal is briefly following the course of the River Fleet which is flowing some seven metres beneath us. Much of the housing on both sides of the canal are conversions of the warehouses and factories which used to line the banks and were one of the centres of London's light industry. There were plenty of firms specialising in food production or furniture making to supply London's burgeoning population.

After about twenty minutes walk from Camden you reach the bridge at Camley Street. Walk up the stairs then cross over the canal and in a hundred metres or so, just past the Coroner's Court, steps on your right take you into the churchyard of St Pancras Old Church. This is surely one of the most atmospheric and historic places in London.

Stop 12

We start with the graveyard.

In front of you as you enter there is the grave of Mary Wollstonecraft, Regency writer, agitator, philosopher and the first recognisably English feminist. Author of 'A Vindication of the Rights of Woman', she was buried with her anarchist partner, William Godwin. Mary died shortly after giving birth to her daughter, also named Mary. It was over the grave of her mother that the younger Mary

planned her elopement with her lover, the poet Percy Bysshe Shelley. As Mary Shelley, she went on to write 'Frankenstein', one of the great Gothick novels of the age.

To the left of Mary Wollstonecraft, an imposing tomb marks the last resting spot of another great Regency figure. This is Sir John Soane, a leading architect of the period and founder of the Soane Museum in Lincolns Inn Fields. His tomb which he designed in the classical style is grade 1 listed (the only other tomb so honoured is Karl Marx's in Highgate) and it served as the inspiration for the red telephone box.

A little further on is a majestic tree, called the Hardy Ash. This commemorates the work of Thomas Hardy who, before he became one of the great authors of the Victorian age, worked in the graveyard supervising the removal of bodies to make way for the rail lines into St Pancras. You'll notice how the roots of the ash have enclosed the tombstones at its base.

To your right is the church of St Pancras.

Stop 13

This has been very heavily restored by the Victorians however some believe that this could be based on the oldest church in London dating back to Roman times. The evidence is scanty but St Pancras, an early Christian martyr, was a popular figure with the Roman army and some believe that the church could have been built on the site of a Roman encampment around 314AD. What is true is that Roman tiles have been used in the building of the church. Some can be seen where the plaster has been stripped back on the north wall. There are some beautiful seventeenth century memorials in the church as well as a seventh century Saxon altar stone.

Exit the church and walk towards the memorial in the centre of the church yard. This commemorates those buried in the graveyard some of whose graves were removed or destroyed as the railways encroached. Many of them were foreigners or refugees as this graveyard was one of the few which allowed the burial of Catholics. The memorial was the work of a remarkable Victorian woman, Angela Burdett-Coutts. Enormously wealthy, think Coutts Bank, she devoted much of her wealth to philanthropy. Among her many initiatives, she helped found the NSPCC, RSPCA, Columbia Market, the Ragged School movement and social housing across London. She also had time to scandalise polite society by marrying at 67 an American nearly forty years younger than herself.

Beyond the memorial loom the walls of the Victorian workhouse now converted into St Pancras Hospital.

Leave the churchyard where you came in and then turn right under the railway lines which run to St Pancras station. In front of you is the entrance to Camley Street Natural Park. This is a wonderful open space built on the site of an old coal yard. Today it is an oasis of green in the centre of Kings Cross.

Take the bridge to the left of the Park over the canal.

Stop 14

At the top of the bridge pause to look down on St. Pancras Lock with its keeper's cottage which was used to pump water back up the canal. To its left is a Victorian water tower for the steam trains coming out of St. Pancras. The station itself was raised above ground level so the tracks could go over the canal without a steep initial climb. The tracks from neighbouring Kings Cross station go under the canal. Carry on into Coal Drops Yard.

This whole area is the site of a great railway depot where coal was brought into London from the north east. In front of you are some Victorian gas holders where gas was extracted from coal; they are now infilled with luxury flats. As you walk over the bridge you enter a recent development of upmarket shops and restaurants on the site of the depot. You can still see some of the original buildings: the stables, viaducts and offices.

Next to Coal Drops Yard is Granary Square. As its name suggests this was a warehouse for imported grain. It's now home to Central St. Martin's School of Art with regular exhibitions open to the public. All around are places to eat and drink. The relocation of the Art School is part of the transformation of this area of London. By the 1980s, Kings Cross was one of the most rundown parts of London, the light industry that had dominated the area since Victorian times had gone leaving only a centre for rough sleeping, prostitution and drug dealing. Now it has been completely transformed with galleries, museums and concert halls opening and major employers like the Guardian and Google setting up their headquarters there.

Walk down the wide steps back on to the canal and continue walking down the towpath. You pass a remarkable floating bookshop with a great variety of cheap and interesting books. As you pass under the road bridge you will see the remains of gates built into the side of the canal. These were an anti-flood precaution built during the second world war. If a bomb had breached the canal it would have flooded the railway lines into Kings Cross which lie underneath the canal thus disrupting vital supplies. The gates were closed when an air raid was imminent, limiting any flooding.

Stop 15

You are soon walking past Battlebridge Basin, one of the great wharves that lined the canal. On the right hand side of the basin was a beer bottling warehouse. At the far end there was a marmalade maker and on the left brick and stone were imported. You can just see the sign for the London Canal Museum on the left. This is well worth visiting; it is built on the site of an ice warehouse and explains the history of the canals and the ice industry in  Victorian London. Today the basin is also home to Kings Place with its galleries, restaurants and concert spaces.

Continue to walk down the canal. In front of you there is the opening of the Islington Tunnel, almost 900 metres long. The canal builders could no longer follow the natural contours as this would have led them towards the City of London which was already built up. The only way through was under the ridge on which Islington stands. To save costs, no towpath was built along the side of the canal in the tunnel. Originally the horses were led over the hill, through the centre of Islington while the barges were 'legged' through the tunnel, hard and dangerous work. Horse and barge were reunited on the other side of the hill.

You can follow the route of the canal through Islington and rejoin the towpath at Duncan Street. From there it's another six miles to the Thames at Limehouse but our walk ends at the start of the tunnel.

Walk up the steps to find the Caledonian Road and walk south down the Caledonian Road towards Kings Cross. You will find plenty of cafes and pubs en route.

Finally

The nearest station is Kings Cross on the Bakerloo, Circle, Northern, Piccadilly, Victoria, Hammersmith and City and Mainline. You could walk back to the station through the extraordinary development around Kings Cross including Google's HQ or visit the London Canal Museum at 12 New Wharf Road, London N1 9RT.

The highpoint of Victorian London – Albertopolis

London in the nineteenth century was, arguably, the greatest city the world had ever seen. Wealth was pouring in from industry, empire and trade. It was growing more rapidly than at any time in its history sucking people in from all over Britain and beyond: in 1800 its population was around one million. By the end of the century, it was over seven million. This growth was only possible thanks to the arrival of the railways; for the first time in history people could live away from their work. London's boundaries expanded exponentially: in 1800 London ended at Hyde Park and Whitechapel. By 1900 it stretched from Ealing to Barking, with its area growing from fifteen square miles to maybe six hundred.

London is very much a Victorian city and so it can be difficult to summarise all that was happening over such a long period of time which witnessed such rapid change. In this walk we look at what, with hindsight, was the highpoint of Britain's and London's wealth and influence in the world, the Great Exhibition of 1851.

By the 1850s Britain was the world's greatest power. It was at the centre of an enormous empire stretching from Australasia to Canada and from India to the West Indies. At home, the industrial revolution was in full swing with new technology and industries transforming the country. In particular, the railways were speeding up transport, enabling the growth of the suburbs and creating a mass market for manufactured goods.

Presiding over this revolutionary transformation of the country was Victoria and her consort Albert. Albert, although German, was the archetype British Victorian gentleman. He believed in progress, science and education. His campaigns included the abolition of slavery across the world, reforming the university curriculum and trying to ameliorate the conditions of the working class. His special concern was the bringing together of science, art and manufacturing to try and ensure that economic progress was based on good design and benefited society. In order to bring together the best principles of design from across the world, Albert was one of the central movers in the proposal to hold a Great Exhibition in Hyde Park in 1851.

The Great Exhibition brought together 13,000 exhibits from forty five countries. They included telescopes, a voting machine, ceramics, the Koh-i-Noor diamond and mounds of raw materials. The pride of place, however, was for British technology which aimed to demonstrate to the world its superiority. The very building which housed the exhibition was a marvel of the modern age. The Crystal Palace was designed, built and erected in only ten months. It used the latest techniques in glass and steel production and was huge, over 550 metres long by 140 metres wide and so tall it enclosed mature trees.

The exhibition was an enormous success with 6 million people, a third of the population of Britain, visiting the attraction. It made a significant profit of £187,000 enough to purchase a large block of land just to the south of where the Great Exhibition was held. On the site, the Natural History museum, the Victoria and Albert museum, the Science museum, the City and Guilds Institute, the Royal School of Art, the Royal School of Music, the Royal Albert Hall and many other institutions were brought together in a single city block. Today, it is also the home of Imperial College one of the world's leading universities. And so Albertopolis was founded. This was the slightly sarcastic name coined by Victorian newspapers in the 1850s and given to the world's first cultural quarter, what we now call South Kensington. There was a common theme underpinning all these institutions; it was to bring together art, design, science and education to drive forward technological progress in a way which benefited society. Alas, Albert saw very little of Albertopolis. He died in 1861 at the age of 42.

Today Albertopolis is a remarkable exhibition of the tastes and concerns of the Victorians. In particular it is a showcase for Victorian architecture, demonstrating the eclectic and varied styles that were popular at the time. Wikipedia mentions eleven different Victorian styles: Gothic revival. Italianate, Neo classical, Jacobethan, Renaissance, Neo Grec, Romanesque revival, Queen Anne revival, Scots Baronial, Second Empire and the Arts and Crafts movement. Most of them are represented in this small corner of London. Remarkably for an age which saw great innovation and change in almost every area of culture and industry, Victorian architecture was extraordinarily derivative, borrowing from previous ages or from abroad. It is perhaps only the Arts and Crafts movement that can be seen as genuinely innovative and British but that too harked back to an earlier, pre-industrial age. The other architectural styles were all based on other ages and other countries. But this is not to disparage Victorian architecture, it still produced some beautiful and instantly recognisable buildings.

Albertopolis is laid out on a north-south axis, with a straight line linking the Albert Memorial, the Royal Albert Hall, the Royal College of Music, Imperial College and the main entrance to the Natural History Museum. On our walk we will visit all of these sites and more and by the end, we should have a much better understanding of the passions of this remarkable generation.

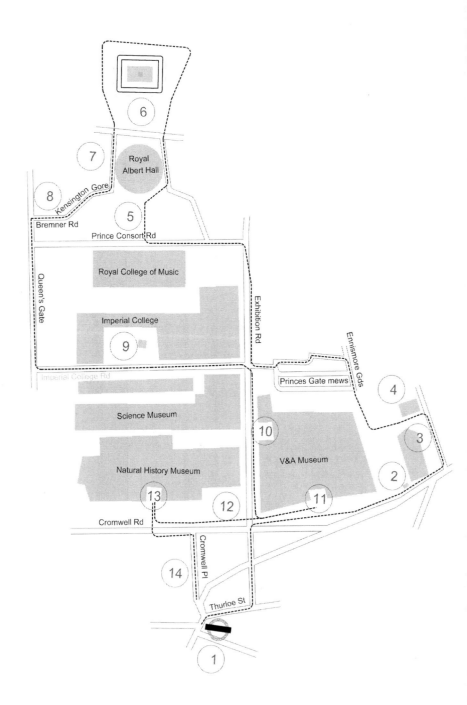

Royal Albert Hall

Kensington Gore

Bremner Rd

Prince Consort Rd

Queen's Gate

Royal College of Music

Imperial College

Exhibition Rd

Ennismore Gds

Princes Gate mews

Imperial College Rd

Science Museum

V&A Museum

Natural History Museum

Cromwell Rd

Cromwell Pl

Thurloe St

Walking Albertopolis

In this walk we are going to trace the impact of Prince Albert and the pioneering generation called the Victorians on the development of London both intellectually and architecturally. On the way we will explore their concerns and passions.

This walk starts at South Kensington Tube Station – main exit (not the Museum exit) and finishes close to South Kensington Tube Station.

Details of what you'll see on this walk start on the page which follows this map...

1 South Kensington Station

2 Cardinal Newman Statue

3 Brompton Oratory

4 Holy Trinity Brompton

5 Albert Statue

6 Albert Memorial

7 Royal Albert Hall

8 Gore Hotel

9 Imperial Institute Entrance

10 Italianate Frontage of V&A

11 Edwardian Redevelopment of V&A

12 Natural History Museum

13 Charles Darwin Statue

14 Home of John Everett Millais

Stop 1

We start at the main exit of South Kensington Station and turn to the right after the ticket barriers. We can stop to admire the intricate Victorian iron work above and within the station. The station opened in 1868 partly to service the developing museum quarter. Originally it was served only by the Metropolitan and District lines. These had been built by the cut and cover method where a trench is built, tracks laid and then the trench is covered over. The Piccadilly Line came some 40 years later and this, like later lines, was built by tunnelling deep underground and laying a tube through the earth along which trains ran. This is why we have two different names, the Underground and the Tube, to describe our transit system. Whatever the method of construction, the railways transformed London by enabling people to live away from their work and to travel quickly across London. In South Kensington, it meant that the specialised museums in Albertopolis could attract people from all over London and beyond.

Head into Thurloe Street, turn right and then turn left into Exhibition Road. This was the road leading to the Great Exhibition of 1851. The beautiful white-painted houses with lots of ornamental stucco around this area mainly date from the 1830s and 40s.

Cross Cromwell Road and walk past the Victoria and Albert Museum. This is where we will end so keep walking past the entrance until you come to a statue on your left.

Stop 2

This is Cardinal John Newman, a key figure in British Catholicism and a very eminent Victorian. Since the Glorious Revolution of 1688 there had been punitive discrimination against Catholics. They were banned from public office, they couldn't vote or own property. These laws were only finally repealed in 1829 on the eve of the Victorian era. Newman was pivotal in making Catholicism respectable. He had been ordained into the Church of England and became prominent in the high church Anglican tradition. In 1845, he with some of his followers joined the Catholic church where he was rapidly ordained and became a cardinal in 1879. His importance to Victorian society was enormous. Newman's very public conversion to Catholicism made it much more respectable and acceptable to society. Newman played a very active role both in the Church helping define what English Catholicism looked like and in secular society, for instance, helping to settle the great Dockers Strike of 1889. In 2019 he was canonised as a Saint by Pope Francis.

Beyond the statue we see the enormous Brompton Oratory.

Stop 3

Newman was interested in the power of the spoken word and became an adherent of St Philip Neri who had created Catholic communities of priests proselytising to their local communities. Newman was instrumental in setting up first the Birmingham Oratory and then in 1854 the Brompton Oratory. The current church was built in 1884 and was the biggest catholic church in England until the construction of Westminster Cathedral. It closely resembles many of the baroque churches built in Rome in the seventeenth century at the height of the counter-reformation. Inside you could be forgiven for thinking you were in Italy, indeed the statues of the apostles that

line the nave were brought from Siena Cathedral. However there is another, hidden side to the Oratory. It is alleged that Kim Philby, one of the Cambridge spies, used to leave messages for his KGB handlers by the altar behind a pillar.

Leave the church and turn left and you reach the church of Holy Trinity Brompton, tucked behind the Oratory. Indeed the church sold the land on which the Oratory is built although they seem to have had second thoughts when they realised just how big and imposing the Oratory was going to be, effectively cutting their church off from the main road.

Stop 4

Consecrated in 1829, this is a good example of Gothic Revival which became very fashionable for church architecture. Adherents of the Gothic Revival movement thought the architecture more spiritual, reflecting a time when the population was more devout. The classicism of Georgian churches was after all based on the architecture of pagan Greece and Rome and allowed little room for spirituality. The church in front of you has all the accoutrements of a medieval church including gargoyles and heads of vaguely medieval kings. The Gothic Revival was one of the major trends in Victorian architecture giving us hundreds of churches, the Houses of Parliament, St. Pancras Station and Tower Bridge among many other buildings.

Holy Trinity is now the headquarters of the Alpha course for evangelical Christians; a very influential wing of the Church of England.

Walk round the church to the left and through the churchyard, enjoying the relative tranquillity of the scene.

Go through the medieval looking gate at the end of the churchyard and turn left along Ennismore Gardens and then into Princes Gate Mews. The pretty little houses along the street betray their original function as stables.

You soon emerge onto Exhibition Road where you turn right, noticing the art deco block of flats which with its clean lines provides a welcome relief from much of the fussiness of Victorian architecture. Continue till you reach Prince Consort Road and turn left past the Jamaican High Commission. Its interest for us is that it is a gorgeous example of Queen Anne Revivalist style. It is built out of red brick which dates it to about 1880 onwards when this style became enormously popular and spread all over London and beyond.

Walk down Prince Consort Road and then walk into the square in front of the Royal Albert Hall towards the statue of Albert on a plinth.

Stop 5

You are now standing on the north-south axis which unites many of the major buildings in Albertopolis from the Albert Memorial, the Albert Hall, the memorial you are standing by, the entrance to the Royal School of Music, the Tower of Imperial College and the entrance to the Natural History Museum.

All around you are examples of Victorian Architecture. To the east are the Albert Hall Mansions, perhaps the best example of Queen Anne Revival. These were the first apartments to be built for the middle and upper classes as until then the London well-to-do had no real tradition of that way of living.

To the south, you have the Royal College of Music; an outpouring of Victorian exuberance with a strange mix of Jacobethan, Flemish Mannerist and Scottish Baronial styles all thrown in together. The School can trace its existence back to the Great Exhibition which provided scholarships to aspiring musicians. A National Training School for Music was set up under the leadership of Arthur Sullivan (of Gilbert and Sullivan fame) but it was not a success and it was replaced by the Royal College of Music in 1883. Since then it has gone from strength to strength with students including Vaughan Williams, Gustav Holst, Benjamin Britten and Andrew Lloyd Weber.

The monument that you are standing next to and surmounted by the figure of Albert commemorates the Great Exhibition. There is a list of all the exhibiting countries and the column details the numbers of exhibitors, visitors and sums raised as well as the worthies who put the monument together. However, the star of the show is Albert and this is whom the column is really about. A plaque on the north side explains that this was supposed just to commemorate the Great Exhibi-

tion but now is dedicated to the 'Good Prince' for his 'far-seeing philanthropy ', 'clear judgement and untiring exertions' which led to 'unprecedented success'.

Walk round the side of the Royal Albert Hall looking at the detailed decoration. Cross Kensington Gore to the Albert Memorial.

Stop 6

The Albert Memorial is one of London's most iconic structures and vividly demonstrates the Victorians' attitudes and concerns. Architecturally, it is high Gothic Revival, based on the Scaliger Tombs in Verona built 500 years before. At its base marble figures represent Europe, Africa, Asia and the Americas with figures at each corner representing the creation of wealth in Agriculture, Commerce, Manufacturing and Engineering. Above them are eight statues of the virtues picked out in gold and murals representing the arts. There are further statues representing the arts and sciences and the central part of the memorial is surrounded by a frieze documenting 169 painters, sculptors, architects, poets and musicians. Of those 169 worthies surrounding Albert, there's just one woman, a female pharaoh credited, apparently incorrectly, with having commissioned a pyramid. At the very centre is a gilded Albert holding not as one might expect the bible but a copy of the catalogue of the Great Exhibition.

The Albert Memorial is a good summary of the concerns and passions of the Victorian upper classes in the middle of the nineteenth century. They wanted to unite art and science, manufacturing and design, tradition with progress. They are all portrayed here in one iconic structure.

Walk back towards the Royal Albert Hall.

Stop 7

This is a very different building from the Albert Memorial. It is not Gothic by any stretch of the imagination. Rather it is a building straight from Classical Rome, a kind of Pantheon in London. Looking up at the frieze which runs round you also realise that this was supposed to be much more than just a concert hall. It was originally called the Central Hall for Arts and Sciences, to bring together the arts and sciences a concept dear to Albert's heart. The frieze commemorates 'The triumph of Arts and Sciences' and commemorates the two being brought together to stimulate manufacturing and construction.

However, over the last century it has specialised as a concert hall with the occasional sporting event. Musically, it has had a chequered history; the acoustics were so poor to begin with that a commentator joked that it was 'the only place where a British composer could be sure of hearing his work twice'. For fifty years it also housed the Central School of Speech and Drama; Judy Dench, Laurence Olivier and Vanessa Redgrave all studied there.

Walk round to the right of the Hall, down Kensington Gore and passing the modern and very ugly Royal College of Art. Suddenly you come across an Italianate mansion decorated with 'putti', fat little children straight out of renaissance Italy. This used to be the headquarters of the Royal College of Organists who moved into the artistic quarter of Albertopolis at the turn of the twentieth century and the house is full of decorative references as to what would be taught inside.

As you bend round Kensington Gore keep an eye out for some beautiful Arts and Crafts tiles inside a doorway. The two women portrayed look like something straight out of a Pre Raphaelite painting, testimony to the only truly native artistic movement of the Victorian age.

Walk down Bremner Road into Queen's Gate. Just on your right is the Gore Hotel at number 192.

Stop 8

The Gore Hotel is a beautiful example of Victorian interior design and normally the administration welcome visitors who may want to look at the entrance hall, lounge, dining room or bar. Much of the decoration is original and dates from the second half of the nineteenth century. It is certainly a treat though perhaps a little pricey to have a cocktail in the bar. The hotel became notorious in 1968 for holding a particularly louche photo shoot with the Rolling Stones on the release of Beggar's Banquet.

Turn left out of the hotel and walk down Queensgate admiring the white stucco houses built in the 1860s on the right and the much more functional buildings of Imperial College on the left. Turn left into Imperial College Road until you reach the white tower guarded by two lions at its foot.

Stop 9

This is all that remains of the Imperial Institute built in 1887 to celebrate Victoria's Golden Jubilee. It was to supposed to be a showcase for the British Empire but never really worked and became offices for government bodies before being demolished to create more space for Imperial College.

Imperial College is now one of the world's leading universities but it too can trace its roots back to the Great Exhibition and Prince Albert. Over the years it brought together many of the institutions supported by the Prince: the Royal College of Science, the City and Guilds and the Royal College of Mines. These were finally amalgamated in 1907 into Imperial College as concern rose that Germany was outstripping Great Britain in scientific education.

Keep walking down Imperial College Road and turn right into Exhibition Road then cross the road to admire the Italianate frontage of the Victoria and Albert museum.

Stop 10

This wing of the museum is named after Sir Henry Cole, a civil servant who amongst his many other accomplishments was the driver behind the Great Exhibition and became the first director of the V&A. (He also designed the Penny Black, sent the world's first Christmas card and was instrumental in setting up the Royal College of Art, Royal College of Music and the institutions that formed Imperial College.) The building itself is an extraordinary recreation of a renaissance Italian palace with wonderful terra-cotta and majolica decoration. Built in 1873, it was the home of the School of Naval Architects, the Science School (headed by Thomas Huxley) and Imperial College before being taken over by the V&A.

The V&A was originally called the South Kensington museum and housed many of the exhibits from the Great Exhibition. Cole saw its function as being 'a schoolroom for everyone' and from the very start its aim was to strengthen education in design. Examples of great work from the past were copied for the next generation of artists, explaining why there are reproductions of Trajan's Column and Michelangelo's David in the museum. It even created a gallery of 'false principles' so students could recognise what was 'bad' art. It was aimed not just at the leisured classes but at the general population. Entrance fees were waived three days a week and it was open in the evening; Cole hoping that it would 'furnish a powerful antidote to the gin palace'.

Walk down the side of the museum, noting the significant bomb damage to the walls and the inscription hailing 'the enduring values of this great museum in a time of conflict.'

Turn left at the Cromwell Road.

Stop 11

By the end of the Victorian century, the South Kensington Museum was renamed the Victoria and Albert Museum as new buildings were constructed along the Cromwell Road and a new main entrance was built. Victorian architecture was being superseded and this new entrance was very much Edwardian in style. Look for the inscription over the main door:

'The excellence of every art must consist in the complete accomplishment of its purpose'. The quote is from Joshua Reynolds but it sums up Albert's philosophy.

Retrace your steps along the frontage of the Museum where statues of the great and good line the facade. Look for those of William Hogarth and Joshua Reynolds. Hogarth was a great painter but better known as an engraver, Reynolds was a renowned portrait painter. Look carefully and you see that Reynolds is not carrying a brush and palette but an engraver's tools. Simply, the two have been mixed up. Even the great Victorians occasionally made a mess of things.

Carry on down Cromwell Road until you reach the front of the Natural History Museum.

Stop 12

This wonderful building is the last great example of nineteenth century architecture that we see on this walk. It is loosely based on the great Romanesque cathedrals of Lombardy but with a very Victorian twist. Everywhere there are decorative flourishes. Birds, animals and lizards are carved into the walls and gates. Most striking

are the sculptures that run high up on the main facade. On the right of the entrance hall are extinct creatures, pterodactyls and sabre toothed tigers. On the left, there are animals of today's world.

This arrangement was due to the predilections of the first director of the museum, Richard Owen. At the time he was most famous for coining the word 'dinosaur' to describe the fossils the museum was collecting. However, he rejected Darwin's theories of evolution and wanted to rebut any links between past and present species so extinct and living animals had to be rigidly separated.

Enter the museum.

Stop 13

Owen visualised the museum as a Cathedral of Learning and inside it does remind one of being in a great church. There are stained glass windows, mosaic floors, cloisters and an ambulatory. Where the altar would be in a church, there is a great statue of Charles Darwin. Clearly, Richard Owen lost the argument on evolution.

It is more than a church, however. Look to the ceiling and you will see steel beams and

glass, reminding you that this was also the time of the building of the great railway termini. The museum effortlessly blends a respect for the past with modern building techniques. Albert would have approved.

Leave the museum and walk down Cromwell Place. Look out for No.7, one of the most famous houses in the history of British art and at the centre of one of the great scandals of the Victorian age.

Stop 14

It was here that the pre-Raphaelite painter John Everett Millais lived with his wife, Effie Gray, who had recently divorced the art critic John Ruskin for the non-consummation of their marriage. Ruskin was one of the great arbiters of Victorian taste, railing against much of the art of the time and his ideas were very influential including with Prince Albert and Henry Cole. He had been friends with Millais and, given that there only a handful of divorce cases each year in the nineteenth century, the circumstances of the case were shocking to respectable society. Eighty years later, the same house became the studio of Francis Bacon, one of the greatest British painters of the twentieth century, who used to supplement his income from holding illegal gambling parties in a back room.

Finally

South Kensington tube is a hundred metres down on the left in Thurloe Street and the area is awash with pubs and cafes. However, to finish your walk in a truly Victorian artistic environment, make your way back to the V&A and enjoy a meal in the cafe surrounded by decorations designed by William Morris in the Arts and Crafts style.

If you're still feeling energetic, West Brompton Cemetery is about 2 kms away. It's a pleasant walk through Victorian apartment blocks and the cemetery is full of interest and contains the grave of Sir Henry Cole, founder of the V&A as well as Emmeline Pankhurst.

The other side of Victorian London
– the East End

The East End has always been different from other parts of London. In the late nineteenth century it gained an almost mythic status; a place of poverty, of darkness, of otherness typified by images of crime and destitution. Today it is a very different place; edgy, arty and dynamic but still the poorest, most diverse part of London.

The concept of the East End has changed over time and there are no agreed or fixed boundaries to the area. It takes in the riverside hamlets of Wapping, Shadwell, Limehouse and Poplar and the key route through it is the old Roman road from Whitechapel, through Stepney, Mile End and Bow. Further north, it includes Shoreditch and Bethnal Green.

The history of the East End for the last three hundred years has been determined by three factors: industry, immigration and impoverishment.

Industry in the East End has always been dominated by the presence of the river and its associated trades; the docks, ship building and maritime supplies. At their peak the London Docks stretched ten miles down the river from the Tower to Woolwich. The last great battleship was built at Thames Iron Works on the Isle of Dogs as late as 1900. Around this area were concentrated all the industries that were too polluting, too noisy or too filthy to be welcomed in the centre of London: this included the refining of whale oil, gas works, brewing, chemicals and ship building. As London expanded in the eighteenth and nineteenth century so the great squares and fine terraces were built in the west end for the rich whilst in the east the housing stock became increasingly reserved for the poor. The very fact that the prevailing winds came from the west meant that smoke and air-borne pollution tended to drift into the east of the City. The Thames too carried its filth downstream from the west to the east. As the docks and railways were built so the housing stock was further depleted forcing the poor into already over-crowded slums.

All kinds of other trades flourished in the east such as clothing, textiles and furniture making. This was in part because it lay outside the boundaries of the City and therefore outside of the control of the Guilds. The Guilds held great power, determining who could work and the regulations for trade. If you were unable to join the guilds then it made sense to work just outside the City, but as close to its markets as possible. Many of these jobs were unskilled, low paid, insecure and subject to downturns in trade.

As a result the East End became the centre for immigration into London. This was partly because of the proximity of the river as the dropping off-point for penniless immigrants, partly because of relatively cheap housing and partly because of industry's demand for unskilled labour. Over the last four hundred years, successive waves of migrants have arrived in the East End, been assimilated into British society and then moved on to other parts of London. One of the first groups to arrive were the Huguenots, French Protestants suffering persecution in their homeland from the 1560s onwards. One of their biggest communities was in Spitalfields where they brought their skills as silk weavers into London. The next two hundred years saw more join them as battles over religion waxed and waned in France. A second wave of migration occurred in the late eighteenth and early nineteenth centuries from Ireland. The building of the great London Docks from 1800 onwards attracted labourers who later became a key part of the dock workforce while Irish weavers joined the textile industry. A third migrant wave arrived in the 1870s and 1880s as Ashkenazi Jews fled persecution in Eastern Europe and found refuge in Whitechapel. Over 150 synagogues were created and many of the streets in the Brick Lane area were almost exclusively Jewish until after the Second World War. From the 1970s onwards, Whitechapel saw the arrival of a fourth great migration: that of Bangladeshis from the Sylheti region. The streets once more became almost monocultural. Mosques were built and the Jewish shops and restaurants were replaced with Bengali names and provisions.

This combination of large scale immigration, poor housing and low paid, insecure work meant that the East End was marked by extreme poverty. By the end of the nineteenth century it was seen as almost a 'Terra Incognita', a place outside polite society. The Whitechapel murders of 1888 shone a spotlight on to the conditions existing in the world's greatest and richest society with books like Jack London's ' People of the Abyss', Arthur Morrison's 'Child of the Jago' or Israel Zangwill's 'Children of the Ghetto' exposing the conditions that existed.

The constant churn of migration led to periodic outbursts of social unrest directed against the latest arrivals. In the early 1900s the British Brothers' League campaigned against the arrival of 'Destitute Foreigners'. In the 1930s the British Union of Fascists under Oswald Mosley were a violent presence in the East End and in the 1970s the National Front were a constant threat on the streets.

There was also a very strong history of radicalism within the East End. The Huguenots had brought with them a tradition of independent thought and had set up 'reading clubs' which became centres of education and discussion. Jewish migrants came often with a tradition of socialist thought and organised themselves into trade unions. The Match Girls strike of 1888 and then the great Dockers Strike the year after introduced mass general unions into Britain. It is not surprising that in the thirties the Communist Party was strong in the East End nor that the great leaders of the Labour Party, George Lansbury and Clement Attlee, were MPs for the area.

Today the area is very different. It is far more diverse, with new waves of incomers re-colonising the area. Brick Lane is no longer mono-cultural even though the street signs are still in Bengali. It is now a centre for street art, cutting edge fashion and tourist shopping. But the poverty and poor housing still remain in the back streets and housing estates.

A walk through the East End

In this walk through the heart of the old East End, we will be exploring the three great themes that defined this area: the industry that the authorities didn't want inside the city walls; the immigration that was attracted to the area over a period of 400 years by the lure of jobs and lastly the impoverishment of its people. One aspect we do not look at is the 'Ripper' murders of 1888; there are far too many books and tours that delve into this appalling episode. This is not one of them.

This walks starts at Liverpool Street Station and finishes at Aldgate East Tube station.

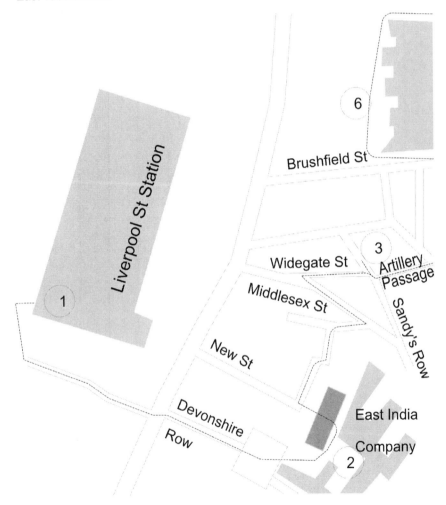

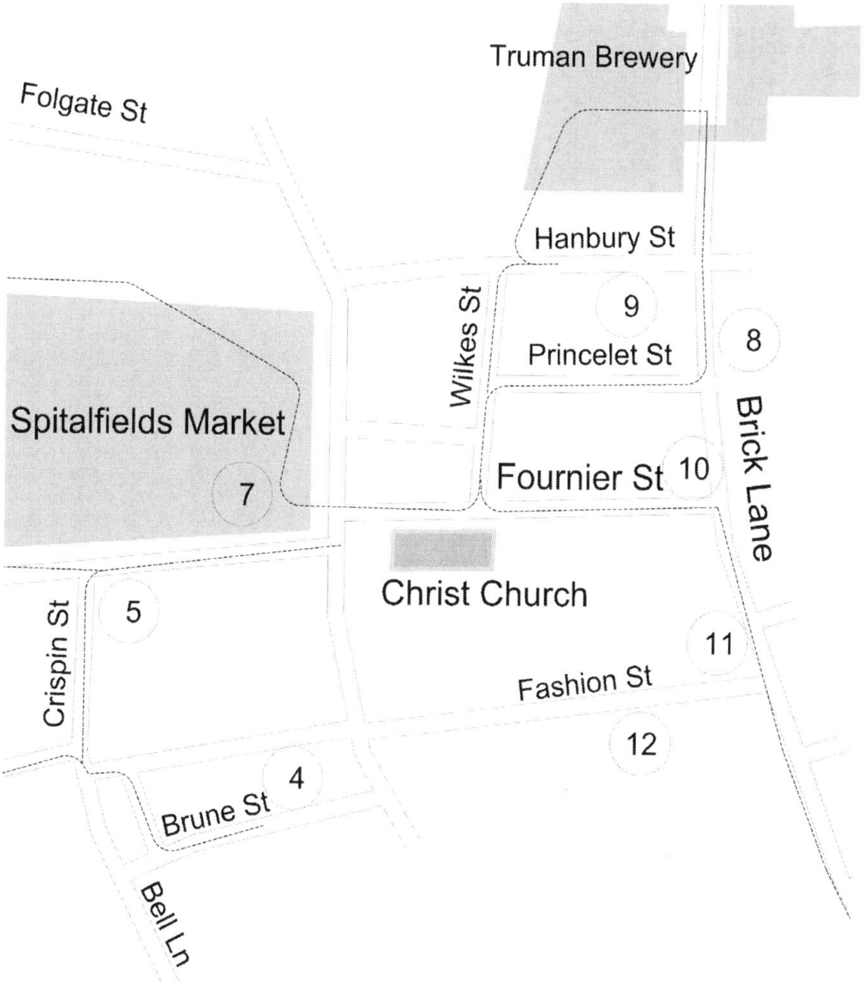

Map (part 1)

1 Liverpool Street Station
2 East India Company
3 Sandy's Row Synagogue
4 Brune Street Soup Kitchen
5 View of ChristChurch
6 Old Charnel House

7 Spitalfields market
8 Brick Lane
9 Hanbury Hall
10 Brick Lane Mosque
11 Christ Church School
12 Fashion Street

Map (part 2)

13 Four Per Cent Industrial Dwellings Company

14 Freedom Press in Angel Alley

15 Whitechapel Gallery

16 Altab Ali Park

17 Whitechapel Bell Foundry

18 East London Mosque and Tower House

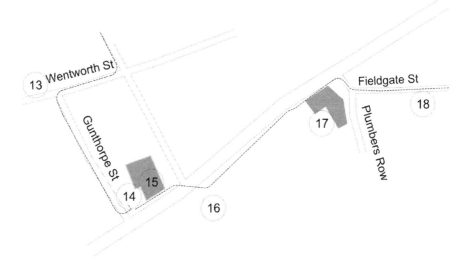

Stop 1

We start inside the concourse of Liverpool Street Mainline Station. The station was built in 1874 and it served as the entry point for many of the immigrants both from abroad or from the provinces who arrived in London. In particular, it saw the arrival of the 'kindertransport', the rescue of some 10,000 Jewish children from Nazi controlled central Europe before the second world war. There are two memorials to the children. The first is by the main entrance to the underground inside the concourse and the second, larger memorial is up the stairs at the back of the station in Liverpool Street, opposite McDonalds. Both statues pack an emotional punch and remind us that the issue of migration has long been a very contentious issue. One of the children saved from the

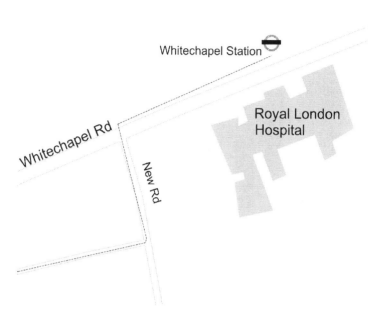

Whitechapel Station

Royal London
Hospital

Whitechapel Rd

New Rd

Nazis, Lord Alf Dubs, has repeatedly agitated to bring unaccompanied child refugees to Britain, so far with very limited success.

Walk to your left down Liverpool Street, noting the plaque marking the site of the Hospital of Bethlehem or Bedlam which from the early 1400s specialised in the care of the mentally ill. Like most hospitals in the medieval period this was built just outside the city walls.

Cross Bishopsgate and walk down Devonshire Row into Devonshire Square, admiring the fine eighteenth century houses. Just after the Square turn to your left and enter the warehouse complex.

Stop 2

These are the great warehouses of the East India Company, built between 1770 and 1820 which at their peak were the biggest warehouses in the world storing all kinds of goods from China and India. 5,000 workers were employed, guarding and distributing the produce that was brought up the newly built Commercial Road from the great docks on the Isle of Dogs. They were effectively sealed off from the outside and highly valuable goods like tea, spices, silks and carpets could be kept safely.

Walk through the complex and take the exit on your left into New Street and turn right outside the Magpie Pub. In front of you notice the fine statue of a Merino Ram at the top of the archway. This is all that

remains of Cooper's Wool Warehouse now being used as office space. Walk towards it then right down Cock Hill and into Catherine Wheel Alley named after a pub which used to stand there and which the famous highwayman, Dick Turpin, was said to have frequented.

Turn left into Middlesex Street. This is the famous Petticoat Lane and has been the site of a Sunday Market for at least 400 years. Named for the clothes that could be bought there, it has been dominated by successive groups of immigrants; Huguenots, Irish, Jews and Bengalis. It has also long been associated with making of clothes and many of the rooms above the shops are still turning out garments. The old name was changed to Middlesex Street around 200 years ago to mark the boundary between the City and the county which surrounded it. Legend has it that Petticoat Lane had too much raciness for the increasingly moralistic nineteenth century so it was changed to a much duller name.

To your left you see a pub, 'The Astronomer'. This used to be the headquarters of the 'Jewish Board of Guardians', set up to administer relief to the poor Jews who flooded into the area from 1880 onwards from Eastern Europe.

Walk right up Widegate Street and turn left into Sandy's Row to stand outside the synagogue.

Stop 3

The Sandy's Row Synagogue is one of only four left in the East End where there used to be over 100. Built in 1766 as a Huguenot chapel, it became a synagogue in the 1870s and is the oldest Ashkenazi place of worship in London.

Retrace your steps and turn left into the atmospheric Artillery Passage. Its name comes from Tudor times when Henry VIII allowed the Fraternity of Artillery to practice on the fields of St. Mary Spital, which, of course, gives us the name Spitalfields.

At the end of the passage you'll see two fine early eighteenth century houses built for a Huguenot family with some of the earliest shop fronts in London. Carry on along Artillery Lane and turn right into Bell Lane.

Across the Lane is Tenter Ground which we walk down. The name comes from cloth making where cloth would be stretched on 'tenter-hooks' to prevent shrinkage, giving us the phrase 'to be on tenterhooks'. Turn left into Brune Street.

Stop 4

There you find the Brune Street Soup Kitchen, set up in 1902 to provide meals for the Jewish poor. At its peak this was providing meals for 5,000 people each week. Note the soup tureen in the centre for those who couldn't read.

Retrace your steps to the corner of Artillery Lane and Bell Lane. This was the site of the Jews Free School from 1822 to the Second World War which at one time with over 4,000 children on roll was the biggest school in the world. In the 1930s children from the Kindertransport would go straight into the school.

Beyond Artillery Lane, Bell Lane becomes Crispin Street. On your left is a Victorian refuge which catered mainly for poor women, note the signs that still exist demarcating the entrances for Women and Men. Walk past the shelter to the corner with Brushfield Street. To your right is the imposing church of Christ Church Spitalfields.

Stop 5

This is one of Nicholas Hawksmoor's great London churches, part of the fifty commissioned by Queen Anne in 1710 to cement the Church of England's position in London. This was especially important in the East End where different shades of non-conformity flourished. Christ Church dominates the area architecturally but its attempts at converting first the Huguenots and then later groups of migrants were very limited. If you have time a visit to the church is very worthwhile. It is one of Hawksmoor's finest churches with a beautifully restored interior. Some of the memorials attest to the efforts made to convert the local Jewish population to Christianity which, in the main, were spectacularly unsuccessful.

Walk back down Brushfield Street along the side of the market. At the corner by the statue of a goat turn right and in a hundred metres or so you will see some stairs leading down to the left.

Stop 6

These lead to a view of the old Charnel House of the Hospital where the dead were buried in the Middle Ages. This burial spot was itself built on the site of a Roman cemetery from the second century. Indeed a spectacular Roman coffin of a young girl was discovered here which can now be seen in the Museum of London. A few steps beyond is a memorial to the latest group of immigrants, refugees from Syria depicted huddled in a tiny boat in which they had travelled to Europe.

A remarkable museum is to be found a few hundred metres further on: Denis Severs' House, a dramatic and artistic recreation of a Huguenot family living over 200 years. It's at No. 18 Folgate Street and, if it is open and you have time, it is well worth a visit.

Otherwise walk into Spitalfields Market.

Stop 7

The market was set up in 1682 and specialised in fruit and vegetables for 300 years. The market moved out to Leyton in the 1990s and was replaced by stalls selling records, antiques, designer clothing and food. While the market is old, the name is much older. Spitalfields reminds us that these were the fields of the hospital of St. Mary, a monastery founded in 1197.

Walk right through and come out on the exit into Commercial Street. Cross it and walk up Fournier Street with the Ten Bells Pub on one side and the church on the other. If you've got a moment, it is worth looking at the fine Victorian tiles in the pub.

Walk down Fournier Street. You pass the graveyard of Christ Church, still often called Itchy Park, thought to derive from the rough sleepers who, with their attendant lice, used to frequent the park. Shamefully, rough sleepers are still there. Unfortunately the name is not the inspiration for the Small Faces song, Itchycoo Park, that comes from a park further east. At No. 2 you see a beautiful house designed in the early eighteenth century by Nicholas Hawksmoor for the priest.

Turn left into Wilkes Street, admiring the fine early eighteenth century Huguenot houses. You'll notice the very large attic windows which housed the weaving looms and aimed to catch as much light as possible enabling longer hours to be worked. Outside some of the houses in Spitalfields you will see wooden bobbins hanging. These signify that they were once owned by weavers.

It's worthwhile peeking into Puma Court on your left. There are some fine eighteenth century houses on the left while on the right there are some tiny Victorian Almshouses for the elderly poor.

Walk up Princelet Street on your right. No. 6-10 used to house a Yiddish theatre called the Hebrew Dramatic Club. It was the site of a terrible tragedy in 1887 when someone called 'fire' and 17 people died in the crush. Just outside you'll see a cast iron plaque in the pavement hinting at past activities. No. 19 is the home of the tiny 'Museum of Immigration'. Open only by arrangement it contains the earliest Ashkenazi synagogue in Britain dating back to 1869. It's housed in a Huguenot home built in 1718.

Next door, a plaque on No. 21 pays tribute to Miriam Moses, the first woman mayor of Stepney.

At the corner of Princelet Street and Brick Lane turn left.

Stop 8

Brick Lane has always been the main street of the Spitalfields area. Named after the medieval brick works, it's been made famous more recently by Monica Ali's bestselling book. At this northern end, Brick Lane is dominated by the enormous Truman's Brewery, dating back to the 1660s. At its peak it employed over 2,000 workers but closed in the 1980s. Today it has been transformed into a warren of shops selling 'vintage' goods and cutting edge fashion, start-up units for tech companies and food stalls from around the world. The area is busy most days but comes to life during the Sunday morning market with young people from all over the world congregating to see and be seen.

Turn left under the bridge into the courtyard and walk through it bearing to your left.

You come out on the corner of Hanbury Street.

Stop 9

On the other side of the street slightly to your left at No. 22 Hanbury Street, you see Hanbury Hall, another old Huguenot Chapel. The Hall was a centre for political and social life for many years. A plaque commemorates the Match Girls' strike of 1888 where support meetings were addressed by the likes of Eleanor Marx and Annie Besant. Charles Dickens often gave readings here of his latest novel.

Outside No. 12 is a plaque recording that this was the birthplace of Bud Flanagan, leader of the 'Crazy Gang', and perhaps best remembered today as the performer of the Dad's Army theme song.

Walk down Wilkes Street and then turn left into Fournier Street. You'll pass an old and faded shop sign, S. Schwarz, at No. 33 which attests to an era when this area was almost completely Jewish. At No. 12 is the studio of Gilbert and George, the noted artists. (Tracy Emin and Rachel Whitehead live nearby).

At the corner of Fournier Street and Brick Lane is one of the most iconic buildings of the East End.

Stop 10

Today this is the Jamme Masjid Brick Lane Mosque, but it was built as a Protestant Huguenot chapel in 1743. Its motto 'Umbra Sumus', We Are All Shadows, on the sundial reminds us of its original purpose. Successively it became a Wesleyan then Methodist Chapel, until in 1898 it was transformed into the Spitalfields Great Synagogue. It is the only building in Britain which has successively hosted the three great Abrahamic religions and is testimony to the changing nature of this extraordinary part of London.

Turn right down Brick Lane. It's always worth popping into Seven Stars Yard which acts as an unofficial open air art gallery with dozens of posters and murals by aspiring artists.

Stop 11

You soon come to Christ Church Primary School. While it is a Church of England school, it catered almost exclusively for Jewish school children from the 1880s to the Second World War. The only sign of this past is the Stars of David on the drain pipes. By the 1970s the school's children were almost entirely of Bangladeshi heritage. Today, the intake is much more diverse with children who can trace their origin from all parts of the world.

Keep walking down Brick Lane. At the time of writing there is some wonderful street art in Heneage Street on your left.

Stop 12

Fashion Street on your right was home to two important Anglo-Jewish writers: Israel Zangwill who wrote 'Children of the Ghetto' in 1892 and Arnold Wesker, who wrote plays such as 'Chicken Soup with Barley' in 1956. On the left hand side of Fashion Street is the facade of an indoor market set up by Abraham Davies in 1905 in a 'Moorish' style. It was a vain attempt to try and coax the outdoor markets inside but rapidly went bankrupt and today houses start-ups and small businesses.

Keep walking down Brick Lane. You're now in the heart of 'Bangla Town', a marketing ploy to attract people to the 'Curry Capital of London'. Nowadays, the curry houses are being interspersed with trendy cafes and there is increasing diversification in the shops and restaurants on the Lane.

Turn right into Wentworth Street and left into Gunthorpe Street.

Stop 13

Just as you turn, you will see a red brick arch. This was the entrance to the Charlotte de Rothschild Four Per Cent Industrial Dwellings Company. Founded by Jewish philanthropists, the initiative was to provide decent, low cost housing for the inhabitants of the East End. The Four Per Cent referred to the rate of return on investment which meant that rents could be affordable at least to those in regular employment. The initiative was very successful and by the turn of the twentieth century, 4,500 were housed in these houses. Only one still survives, it's in Stepney we'll see it on the next walk.

Walk down Gunthorpe Street and you emerge onto Whitechapel High Street.

Look for the Star of David above the shop front at No. 88. This marks where the Jewish Daily Post, a Yiddish newspaper, was published in the 1930s. Follow the map and walk a few metres to the east into Angel Alley.

Stop 14

Freedom Press, a bookshop and publisher, has been based here since 1886, regularly producing Britain's only anarchist newspaper. The mural of radicals includes Rudolph Rocker and Peter Kropotkin who were both based in the East End, the first organising Jewish trade unions the second, a Russian aristocratic exile, founded Freedom Press.

Return to the High Street and next door is the Whitechapel Gallery which also incorporates the Whitechapel Library.

Stop 15

The Gallery has a long history of both nurturing artists from the East End and bringing artists to the area. It has hosted artists as diverse as Jackson Pollock, Mark Rothko, Frida Kahlo, David Hockney, Bridget Riley and Gilbert & George; often introducing them for the first time to the British public. However, it is most famous for 'Guernica', Picasso's masterpiece which was exhibited here in 1939, the only time it has been seen in the UK. It was used to raise money for the Republican side in the Spanish Civil War and those who couldn't afford the admission were encouraged to leave pairs of boots to equip Republican troops and refugees.

A plaque on the wall of the Gallery commemorates Isaac Rosenberg, one of the war poets killed in action in the First World War. He was also a very talented painter and his work is exhibited in the National Portrait Gallery and Tate Britain.

Cross Whitechapel Road. This is the original Roman road linking London with Colchester, the first capital of Roman Britain.

In front of you is Altab Ali Park, named after the victim of a racist attack who was murdered here in 1978. Enter the park noting the old water fountain.

Stop 16

This is the churchyard of the original White Chapel. In the thirteenth century, a chapel of ease was built here so travellers could give thanks for a safe arrival in London or to offer prayers before setting off. Painted white it became the White Chapel and gave its name to the area. The church was destroyed in the Blitz although its ghostly outline can still be traced.

Continue walking along the Whitechapel Road, you soon arrive at the front of the Whitechapel Bell Foundry.

Stop 17

Until its closure in 2018, this was the oldest manufacturing company in the UK. It could trace its origins back to 1420 and had been in Whitechapel since 1570. Its most famous bells were Big Ben in the Palace of Westminster and the Liberty Bell in Philadelphia, the symbol of the American Revolution.

Walk up Plumbers Row and cross into Fieldgate Street.

Stop 18

You are walking at the back of the great East London Mosque and much of this end of the street is taken up with philanthropic Islamic institutions. However, remnants of older institutions remain. Watch out for the sign of the Fieldgate Street Great Synagogue founded in 1899.

A little further on is a great brick building, Tower House. This was built as cheap lodgings for working men in 1902 and was a landmark for many years. Famous tenants include Jack London who stayed here while researching 'People of the Abyss', George Orwell when writing 'Down and Out in Paris and London' and Josef Stalin while attending the Bolshevik conference held nearby in 1907 along with Lenin and Trotsky.

Continue down Fieldgate Street, past the famous Tayyabs restaurant, and turn left down New Road until you reach Whitechapel Road once more. New Road becomes Vallance Road famous as the childhood home of Ronnie and Reggie Kray. We turn right down Whitechapel Road in front of The Royal London Hospital.

In a few hundred metres there are signs to Whitechapel tube station, the end of our walk.

Victorian philanthropy in Whitechapel and Stepney

We have already seen how much of the East End was character-ised by grinding poverty especially at the end of the nineteenth century. There had always been sporadic attempts to improve the lot of the poor in the area; the church, the guilds, immigrant groups and charities had all made a contribution over the years. It was the Whitechapel murders of Jack the Ripper which shone a spotlight into this quarter of London and polite society was horrified by what had been revealed. The East End was characterised by squalor, poverty and degradation. Efforts to ameliorate living conditions were redoubled and the East End became one of the great centres of social reform. Traces of this history can be seen throughout Whitechapel and Stepney.

Historically, the monasteries based in the East End had provided some form of help to the poor especially in the form of medical care. There had been two monasteries in the East End, St. Katherine's just to the east of the Tower of London now covered by St. Katherine's Dock and St. Mary's Hospital, just to the north of Bishopsgate. It was the fields of St Mary's that are today commemorated as Spitalfields. The dissolu-tion of the monasteries ended provision of hospital services in the east for two hundred years. It was not until 1740 that a group of concerned individuals opened the London Infirmary, originally in Moorfields but within a few years it moved to new premises on the Whitechapel Road where it remains to this day.

Other forms of charitable work were also provided by parishes, the guilds of London or sometimes great companies who set up alms-houses for the old and charity schools for the young. In particular after the Whitechapel murders of 1888 there was a focus on the provision of better housing by clearing the worst of the slums. Great housing charities funded by Guinness, Peabody and Rothschild created the 4% Industrial Dwellings. They were so called because the rents had to pay a dividend of 4% on the original capital cost. These dwellings meant an enormous improvement on the housing stock providing decent, if cramped, accommodation for those in steady work.

The East End was home to successive waves of immigrant groups and each of them often had to rely on their own efforts to survive in their new home. The first group to impact on the East End were Jews who returned to London on the invitation of Oliver Cromwell nearly 400 years after their expulsion by Edward I. The first arrivals were Sephardic Jews, based in Amsterdam but originating from Spain and Portugal. They built a synagogue just on the City's walls at Bevis Marks, the oldest synagogue in continuous use in Europe. The commu-nity also provided cemeteries in which the community could bury its dead. There are a number of cemeteries along the Whitechapel Road. The Sephardic community created the Velho (Old) Cemetery in 1657, while the Ashkenazi created the Alderney Road Cemetery forty years later. When the Velho reached capacity, the Nuevo (New) Cemetery was set up in 1724, a few hundred metres to the east. The tradition of Jewish self-help came to the fore with the arrival of 150,000 Jews from Eastern Europe between 1870 and 1905. Schools, hospitals, old people's homes and soup kitchens were set up sometimes with significant contributions from the established Jewish community to help the Ashkenazi immigrants.

A very different kind of help was provided by the charities that were set up in the area during the nineteenth century. Philanthropists often inspired by Christianity created charities and movements to alleviate the worst of the despair. Unfortunately some of their Christian virtues were not always manifest in their dealings with each other as there was intense and bitter rivalry at times between them. There were hundreds of different initiatives in the East End at the time but three will illustrate their scope and concerns.

Frederick Charrington was heir to the family's brewery in the East End but after witnessing a drunken man emerging from one of Charrington's pubs and assaulting his wife he gave up his fortune. Instead he devoted himself to ridding the East End of the twin evils of alcoholism and prostitution. At great personal risk he closed down dozens of brothels in Whitechapel and campaigned for temperance against alcohol. He set up the Tower Hamlets Mission on the Mile End Road and built the Great Assembly Hall which could seat 5,000 people. Later he bought Osea Island off the Essex coast to provide a treatment centre for addicts. The mission still survives today providing support to drug users and the homeless.

Thomas Barnardo came to London from Dublin to train in medicine to become a missionary in China. Moved by the plight of children in the East End he abandoned his studies and his vocation to found a series of children's homes and schools for the neglected youngsters of the area. The first was set up in 1867 when he was only 22. By the time he died 96 institutions were looking after 8,500 children every year. He was subjected to significant abuse by Charrington who accused him of kidnapping children, doctoring before and after photographs of children he rescued and, in one particularly salacious case, of sexual impropriety.

William and Catherine Booth founded the Salvation Army in the East End to combat ignorance, drunkenness and immorality. Organised along semi-military lines it campaigned throughout London against those evils but also set up hostels, soup kitchens and aid to the poor. According to William Booth "The 3 S's best expressed the way which the Army administered to the 'down and outs': first, soup; second, soap; and finally, salvation". In its early years the Salvation Army faced ferocious opposition with its adherents being attacked and even killed in battles with the 'Skeleton Army', a mob funded by the brewers and publicans. The Booths were also accused of misusing funds, promoting women into men's work and creating a structure based on nepotism. The last was perhaps true as both Bramwell and Evangeline Booth succeeded their father as General of the Salvation Army. Despite these criticisms the Army boomed and now has a membership of 1.7 million in 131 countries.

While the new mass charities had a significant impact on living conditions for some in the East End they mainly dealt with those at the very bottom of society. They also tended to concentrate on the outcomes created by destitution whether it be prostitution, child abandonment or alcoholism rather than on the root causes of poor housing, poor employment and poor education. For that, state intervention was needed.

One of the many missions remaining in the East End is a place called Toynbee Hall. Its vision was to create a place for leaders of the future to work in the East End so they could see the problems which needed addressing at first hand. Among the volunteers at the beginning of the twentieth century were two young Oxford graduates: William Beveridge and Clement Attlee. The latter became MP for Limehouse in 1922. Between them they were the key architects of the Welfare State in post war Britain as Beveridge wrote his famous report and Attlee implemented it with the National Health Service, National Insurance, National Assistance and the building of council homes.

The East End was also the centre of Municipal Socialism where the local councils took the initiative in ameliorating poor housing and poverty. Their greatest achievement was perhaps the creation of good solidly built houses at affordable rents; however, they also took the initiative in combating unemployment. This culminated in the Poplar Rates Revolt of 1921 where the entire council were imprisoned for refusing to pay money to central government funds using them instead for the relief of poverty in the East End.

The East End is full of reminders of 400 years of philanthropy, self-help and organisation and while many challenges remain today the appalling conditions of the late nineteenth century are mercifully gone.

Philanthropy in the East End – the walk

In this walk we explore a different side of the East End to Spitalfields. It's less well known and much less fashionable but equally fascinating with some remarkable buildings, memorials and museums.

Walk starts at Whitechapel Tube Station and finishes at Stepney Green Tube Station

From Whitechapel tube follow the signs to the Royal London Hospital and Whitechapel Road. Whitechapel Road hosts one of the oldest and most vibrant daily food markets in London. Specialising in Bangla Deshi foodstuffs and textiles it is unique and well worth spending a few minutes exploring.

Walk to your right to the pedestrian crossing.

1 Working Lads Institute

2 Hospital Museum

3 Trinity Almshouses

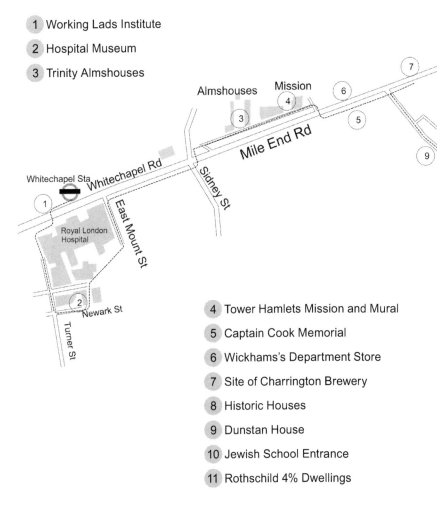

4 Tower Hamlets Mission and Mural

5 Captain Cook Memorial

6 Wickhams's Department Store

7 Site of Charrington Brewery

8 Historic Houses

9 Dunstan House

10 Jewish School Entrance

11 Rothschild 4% Dwellings

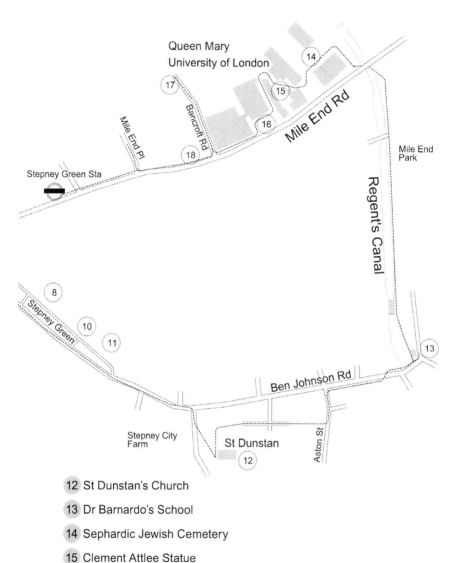

12 St Dunstan's Church

13 Dr Barnardo's School

14 Sephardic Jewish Cemetery

15 Clement Attlee Statue

16 People's Palace

17 Ashkenazi Cemetery

18 Albert Stern House

Stop 1

Before you cross, look at two buildings behind you. On the facade of the first you can see the ghostly remnants of its previous use: a Working Lads Institute dating from the late nineteenth century. It was there to provide wholesome pursuits for boys and young men after they had finished work. You can still see the signs for the lecture hall and gymnasium, providing a healthy mind in a healthy body.

Its near neighbour at number 259 is now a jewellers and sari shop but in the 1880s it was where 'The Elephant Man', Joseph Merrick was exhibited to the public as part of a freak show. He was rescued by a surgeon at the London Hospital where he spent the last few years of his life before dying at the age of 28. There's also a monument to Edward VII donated by the Jewish inhabitants of the East End as he had friends amongst the Sephardic Jewish Community which helped ease some of the rampant anti-Semitism of that era.

Cross Whitechapel Road and turn to your right. In front of you is the facade of the Royal London Hospital. Founded in 1740 and moving to the Whitechapel Road in 1757, it brought health treatment to generations of East Londoners. Before then there were no public hospitals operating in the East End despite its rapidly growing population. The original building now houses the council offices of Tower Hamlets Council after an enormous new hospital was built just behind it.

Walk west towards the City and then turn left into Turner Street and walk through the old buildings of the Hospital. Take a left at Newark Street admiring the beautiful early Victorian 'Gothick' houses. On your left you come to the entrance to the museum of the hospital; one of the most atmospheric little museums in London.

Stop 2

The museum is well worth a visit. It illustrates the development of the hospital over the last 250 years and more. It also tells the story of two of the most famous people associated with the hospital, Joseph Merrick and Edith Cavell, the nurse shot by the Germans at the start of the First World War. There is much to look at; in particular, how hospital treatment has developed over the last three hundred years. But look out also for an early painting of the hospital. Next to it, there is an imposing 'hill'. In fact this is the remnant of a fort built in the Civil War to defend Parliamentarian London from attack by the forces of Charles I. It is still remembered in the name of Mount Street nearby.

Leaving the museum continue down Newark Street then turn left through the new hospital and walk down East Mount Street to rejoin the Whitechapel Road. Turn right and walk eastwards. Across the road is the facade of the old Mann Crossman & Paulins Brewery. This was one of the big local employers but the presence of the great brewers as well as the hundreds of pubs in the area were to become a focal point of opposition for the growing Temperance Movement of the late nineteenth century. One of the most notorious pubs is just next door. The Blind Beggar is where Ronnie Kray shot and killed George Cornell, a rival gangster, in 1966. At the time police could find no witnesses. Within a few years half the East End claimed to be there that night.

At the lights cross Sidney Street and then Whitechapel Road to stand on the diagonal corner. Sidney Street achieved national fame in 1911 when a group of Latvian revolutionaries who had shot three policemen in a bungled robbery were tracked down to rooms there. 'The siege of Sidney Street' ensued, directed by the then Home Secretary Winston Churchill. The cornered gang members all died when the house they were sheltering in caught fire.

You are now standing in Mile End Waste. This patch of ground has a long history dating back centuries. This was where the young king Richard II gave in to the demands of the peasants revolt in 1381 before reneging a few days later at Smithfield. Fast forward 500 years and the Waste was at the centre of the philanthropic efforts to relieve the plight of the poor.

Stop 3

You walk past a statue of William Booth to arrive after a hundred metres or so at the Trinity Almshouses, proof that philanthropic efforts have always been part of East End life. Built in 1695 by Trinity House, they were for '28 decay'd masters and commanders of ships or ye widows thereof'.

The east side of the alms-houses houses the Tower Hamlets Mission set up by Frederick Charrington. It was here that he built his enormous Great Hall which could seat 5,000 and provided uplifting activities for local people. The mission continues to this day providing care and accommodation on its original site.

Stop 4

On the side of the building just east of the almshouses there is a mural painted on the side of a wall detailing some of the characters that have been prominent in the area. They include the Kray twins, the Queen, David Hockney and Lenin chatting to the Elephant Man.

There are two memorials on the roadside to William and Catherine Booth, founders of the Salvation Army. It was here William began preaching to East Enders about the gospel and the evils of alcohol. The Blind Beggar, over the road, was a favourite target and unsurprisingly violence often erupted. The Salvation Army is still active in the area providing food and shelter to the homeless in a large hostel back on the Whitechapel Road.

Stop 5

Cross Mile End Road on to the south side and a few metres down to the east you can see a memorial to Captain Cook on the site of his London house. It details his many explorations spanning the east and west coasts of Canada, Australia and New Zealand.

The plaque reminds us that in the eighteenth century Stepney was a place of some wealth, home to many of the ships' captains who were exploring the world and creating the British Empire. We will see some of the grand houses later in the walk.

Stop 6

Look across the road to spot a grand classical building with a small white building squeezed in the middle. This was Wickham's Department Store, dubbed the 'Selfridges of the East'. The owners planned a great classical building running along the road. Unfortunately for them they had forgotten about the Spiegelhalter family. Originally from Germany, the jewellery family would not sell up. As a result, the Wickhams had to build their grand new shop around them. The Spiegelhalters outlived the Wickhams only closing in 1982.

Next door is the Genesis Cinema, built on the site of an old music hall. It premiered 'Sparrows Can't Sing' with Barbara Windsor in the lead role. It was the highpoint of the Krays' power and notoriety; they hosted the after film party and ensured a good turnout with East Enders lining the streets waving union jacks as the stars arrived. Guests included the Earl of Snowdon, Princess Margaret's husband. Margaret diplomatically pulled out, claiming she was indisposed.

Stop 7

Walk a little further down Mile End Road and you are standing outside what remains of the great Charrington brewery, one of the biggest in London and from which Frederick Charrington broke. A little further on you arrive at a beautiful terrace dating from the early eighteenth century which once belonged to the Charrington family.

Retrace your steps, cross the road and walk into Stepney Green. This leads to the parish church of St. Dunstan's and as you walk down the road, the hustle of the Mile End Road gradually recedes and you find yourself in a different, quieter and older London.

Stop 8

Walk through the gardens which give the street its name. On your left are some beautiful houses dating back to the end of the seventeenth century. One house built in the 1690s, number 37, became a pharmacy and then an old people's home as part of the philanthropic effort amongst the Jewish community two hundred years later.

Stop 9

On the other side of the Green you will see a massive red brick housing block. This is Dunstan House built by Christian philanthropists. This is an example of one of the 4% buildings, so called because the rent was supposed to give a return of 4% on the capital costs. The housing was revolutionary for the East End, providing running water and gas lighting for the first time. However, the need for a return on investment did mean that the very poorest couldn't afford them and there was pressure to squeeze as many flats as possible into the available space.

Stop 10

Back on your left hand side, you pass the gates to the Stepney Jewish School where you can spot the green monogram which is still there despite the school closing after the Second World War as the Jewish population moved north and east.

Stop 11

Shortly after the school is another example of a 4% Industrial Dwelling. The company concerned with this house was chaired by Nathaniel Rothschild, friend of Edward VII, and catered for the Jewish community.

Walk to the end of the Gardens and continue past Stepney City Farm which offers you the slightly incongruous view of a flock of sheep in the middle of the city. It's a timely reminder that East End charitable enterprises are still flourishing in the twenty first century.

As you walk past the farm you come to the parish church of St. Dunstan and All Saints.

Stop 12

This is one of the most historic of London churches, dating back to around 950 and probably replacing an earlier wooden church. Most of the exterior, though restored over the ages, is from the fifteenth century and looks for all the world like a rural medieval church snuggling in the countryside. For many years it was the only church in East London and served an area from the City to Barking. It was from this 'Mother Church' that Chapels of Ease such as at Whitechapel were licensed. The church flies the Red Ensign symbolising the fact that the church registers all those born at sea into the parish records.

Inside, the church is beautiful with an Anglo-Saxon Rood and a Norman font. It is a tranquil and beautiful place in the middle of the bustle of the East End.

Come out of the church and walk out of the graveyard and then immediately right down the passageway to its side leading to Durham Row. You pass some old houses probably shops in the Victorian era. Turn left, then immediately right down Elsa Street. At the end of the street there is a fine example of inter-war council housing. Blocks of flats like these exist all over London. They were built to a very high standard and provided working people with good, well-built homes, often for the first time.

Turn left down Aston Street and then right on to Ben Johnson Road. Cross over the canal bridge and on your left is the remarkable Ragged School Museum.

Stop 13

This was the largest of Thomas Barnardo's ragged schools in London where slum children could gain a free education. Founded in 1877 it educated tens of thousands of children over the years. Today it contains a moving museum where original photos show the awful poverty that existed at the time. It also hosts school visits where children experience how  classes were run in the late nineteenth century. Do check the opening hours and days as it relies on dedicated volunteers to stay open. (See the www.raggedschoolmuseum.org.uk)

When you have finished in the museum go back to the canal, go down the steps to the towpath and walk past the back of the museum heading north.

This is the Regent's Canal, which we visited on our Regency walk further to the west. The canal links the docks at Limehouse with the Midlands and North. It supplied the industries of the East End with the raw materials they needed and this whole area was heavily industrialised. Few traces of the old manufacturing industry remain. Today the area has been transformed into an urban park and the towpath attracts cyclists and joggers.

After about a quarter of mile the canal goes under the Mile End Road. Immediately after the bridge, go up the stairs on the right then turn right along the road. In a few metres enter the grounds of Queen Mary University of London on your right. Queen Mary's brought higher education into the East End and it traces its history back to the London Hospital's training school which became the People's Palace Technical School and finally became a college within the University of London. Walk to your left through the campus.

Stop 14

Continue through the grounds until you come to one the most extraordinary sights in any University; the Betahayim Nuevo.

This is the 'New' Sephardic Jewish Cemetery founded in 1725. The Jewish community had been invited back to England by Oliver Cromwell in the 1650s, 360 years after their expulsion by Edward I in 1290. The Sephardic community who originated from Spain and Portugal but were mainly based in Amsterdam were the first to arrive. They settled in the City of London and went on to found the Bevis Marks Synagogue, the oldest in Britain. The community was given a plot of land outside the City walls to bury their dead. This was the Velho, the 'Old' Cemetery which we will see a little later on the walk. Once this was full, the 'New' cemetery was created and was still being used into the twentieth century. Look carefully at the grave stones and you will see that many of the names emanate from the Mediterranean indicating their Sephardic origins.

Stop 15

Continue through the University.

You soon come to a statue of perhaps the greatest social reformer of them all – Clement Attlee. He is portrayed with a weighty tome in his hand. It is a copy of the National Assistance Act which transformed living conditions for the working class in Britain after the Second World War. His government also introduced the National Health Service, National Insurance and family allowances as well as bringing key industries under state control. The Labour Government of 1945 marked a significant shift in policy regarding the alleviation of poverty; charity was no longer enough, the state had to take responsibility. As Attlee put it: 'Charity is a cold grey lifeless thing. If a rich man wants to help the poor, he should pay his taxes gladly, not dole out money on a whim'.

Walk into Library Square and then take a left along the side of the People's Palace until you once again reach the Mile End Road.

Stop 16

The People's Palace was one of the great philanthropic institutions of the East End. It opened in 1887 and brought education and entertainment to the community. There was a great concert hall, an exhibition space, a huge library with space for 250,000 books, a swimming pool and gymnasium as well as classrooms for a Technical School. It was an enormous success with 1000 people using the library every day and 5,500 students were enrolled in the Technical School. Much of the original building was destroyed in a catastrophic fire and rebuilt in the 1930s where it formed the basis for Queen Mary's College. The clock tower dates from the 1890s while the Great Hall is 1930s Art Deco. Look for the frieze around the outside created by Eric Gill which illustrates some of the activities such as sport, music and dance that can be found inside.

Continue to walk down Mile End Road and turn right into Bancroft Road. You first pass the Tower Hamlets Local History Library which contains much information about the East End and then reach Mile End Hospital. The grand red brick building at its centre is the old workhouse for the area. This was the primary form of 'charitable' relief for the poor in the nineteenth century. Ending in the workhouse usually meant families being split up, poor living conditions, inadequate food and harsh manual labour. It was little wonder that many preferred abject poverty and semi-homelessness than entry to these dreaded institutions.

Stop 17

A few hundred metres along Bancroft Road brings you to an old Ashkenazi cemetery. In the nineteenth century this was owned by a synagogue in Covent Garden but fell into disuse and was damaged in the Blitz. The Ashkenazi Jewish community from Eastern Europe started arriving in London in the early eighteenth century although it was only in the 1870s that repression in the Russian empire led to mass Ashkenazi immigration into London.

Retrace your steps to once again reach the Mile End Road. Turn right to reach Albert Stern House.

Stop 18

This is a remarkable early eighteenth century house which for many years was at the heart of Sephardic charitable efforts in the area. It has been an old people's home and a maternity hospital for the Jewish community. At the back of the house lies the Betayim Velho, the oldest Sephardic cemetery which can only be visited by prior appointment.

Walk 25 metres further along Mile End Road and turn right through the arch into Mile End Place. This is a beautiful little oasis of nineteenth century cottages which seem to be a

very long way from the hustle of the main road. Its peace may come from the fact that it is surrounded by cemeteries: the wall at the end of the street seals off the Ashkenazi cemetery of Alderney Grove while over the wall to your right is the Sephardic Betayim Velho.

Finally

This is the end of the walk. A few hundred metres further down Mile End Road will bring you to Stepney Green Underground Station. There are restaurants mainly of the fried chicken variety on the High Road but you might find it interesting to drop into the Half Moon Pub which is housed in a Methodist Chapel and has an interesting history as a centre for radical theatre.

Literary London and the Bloomsbury Set

London in the first half of the twentieth century was changing rapidly. The certainties of the Edwardian era of British dominance in an ordered world had ended on the battlefields of France. The Russian Revolution and the rise of Italian Fascism meant that the old ways of ruling were being challenged. In Britain the Labour Party had not only been formed but had been in government, albeit briefly. Women had finally won the vote after years of struggle and their impact on society, arts and politics was becoming increasingly important.

This intellectual ferment was focussed on a small area of central London – Bloomsbury and Fitzrovia. It had been home to generations of artists and intellectuals, most notably to the Bloomsbury Set, who were at the forefront of the artistic and political debate of the first half of the twentieth century.

The Bloomsbury and Fitzrovia that we know today is mainly a product of the Regency building boom at the beginning of the nineteenth century. The first square, Bloomsbury, had been laid out after the Restoration in 1660 by the Earl of Southampton. He had built himself a great mansion just to the north. This was then the edge of London and the new development attracted many because of its clean air and open aspect. The land passed to the Bedford family in 1667 and 130 years later the same family transformed the whole area. Employing the renowned Regency architects, Decimus Burton and John Nash, great squares were built from 1800 onwards with wide avenues linking them. The Bedford family's other titles or associated names Include Russell, Woburn, Tavistock and Gordon. It was lucky they had so many titles because there were an awful lot of squares and streets to name.

The development was a great success attracting the solid respectable middle classes. During the nineteenth century, its attractiveness increased with the creation of two great Victorian institutions; the British Museum in the south and University College to the north. The area became known for its intellectual life as writers, academics and artists moved in replacing, in part, lawyers, doctors and businessmen. Fitzrovia was less refined and a bit more down market as it shared its spaces with shops and some manufacturing industry. During the nineteenth century the area was home to a tradition of non-conformity, radicalism and bohemianism. Simon Bolivar, Charles Dickens, Karl Marx, Vladimir Lenin, Oscar Wilde, George Bernard Shaw and assorted groups of anarchists, mainly from the continent, all made their home there.

It was in this area that the 'Bloomsbury Set' emerged at the turn of the twentieth century. It revolved around two sisters, Virginia and Vanessa Stephen and their brothers' friends from Cambridge, Leonard Woolf, Lytton Strachey, Clive Bell, EM Forster and John Maynard Keynes. They were joined by two painters, Duncan Grant and Roger

Fry. Virginia married Leonard and Vanessa married Clive but this was not the end of their affairs: as Dorothy Parker pointed out 'They lived in squares, painted in circles and loved in triangles.' Indeed it was much more complex than that: Duncan Grant, for instance, had sexual relationships with Lytton Strachey, J. M. Keynes and a long relationship with Vanessa with whom he fathered a child.

Many more intellectuals and free thinkers were on the periphery of the group. These included Bertrand Russell, the leading philosopher of the age and a member of the Bedford family, Lady Ottoline Morrell, the literary hostess, T. S. Eliot, the poet, Katherine Mansfield and Vita Sackville-West, both authors.

The main concerns of the Bloomsbury Set were above all aesthetic; a strong belief in art for art's sake, the value of intellectual pursuits and personal fulfilment especially through relationships. Politically they were on the left and socially very liberal. As one of their number said 'To say they were unconventional suggests deliberate flouting of the rules; it was rather they were quite uninterested in conventions, but passionately in ideas'.

Their individual achievements were wide ranging and long lasting. Virginia Woolf is still considered to be one of most important modernist authors of the twentieth century and her books such Mrs Dalloway, A Room of One's Own or Orlando are still read. E. M. Forster is also recognised as a great British novelist having been nominated for the Nobel Prize for Literature on sixteen separate occasions for works such as A Room with a View, Howards End and A Passage to India. J. M. Keynes became the pre-eminent economist of the twentieth century as well as being the driving force behind the World Bank, the IMF and the Arts Council. In the field of art Duncan Grant, Vanessa Bell and Roger Fry created a recognisably English twentieth century art.

While their individual legacies remain, it is, perhaps, their combined work and intertwined lives that reverberate more. They broke decisively with Victorian morality, deference and conventionality. The Bloomsbury Set raised issues about aesthetics, feminism, sexuality, relationships and family which we still discuss and grapple with today.

The Bloomsbury Set ended with the Second World War but the literary and artistic tradition continued. Neighbouring Fitzrovia became the drinking place of a new generation of writers and artists. Augustus John, Jacob Epstein, Wyndham Lewis, Dylan Thomas, Quentin Crisp and George Orwell all lived and drank in the area in pubs like the Fitzroy Tavern and the Wheatsheaf. The tone of much of this new generation was very different from the old ethereal Bloomsbury set. It was gritty, committed politically and more bohemian. The area reflected these concerns: Fitzrovia was never as genteel as Bloomsbury. Even today it has a much more lived in feel.

Today, Fitzrovia has been much developed but the great Bloomsbury squares remain as Virginia Woolf would have known them. Together, they make a fascinating London neighbourhood, full of hidden gems as well as glimpses of a once flourishing literary world.

Walking with the Bloomsberries

In this walk we see where the Bloomsbury Set lived, loved and worked discovering as we go a rich intellectual tradition spanning two hundred and fifty years of literary history.

Walk starts at Holborn Tube Station and finishes at Tottenham Court Road Tube Station. Exit Holborn Tube and diagonally cross both roads to the opposite corner. Walk northwards and then turn down the imposing Sicilian Avenue to reach Bloomsbury Square.

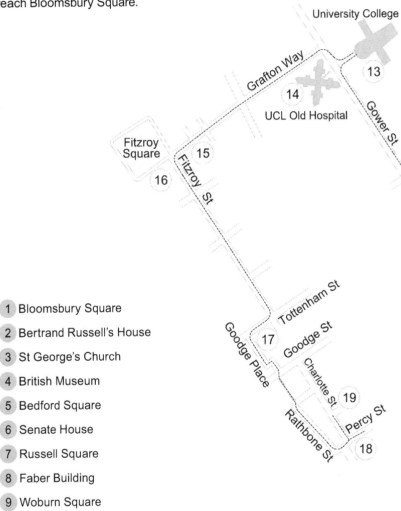

1 Bloomsbury Square

2 Bertrand Russell's House

3 St George's Church

4 British Museum

5 Bedford Square

6 Senate House

7 Russell Square

8 Faber Building

9 Woburn Square

10 Tavistock Square

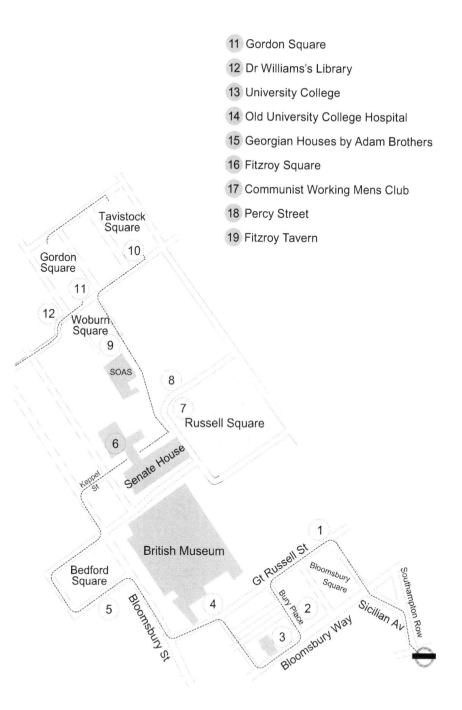

11 Gordon Square
12 Dr Williams's Library
13 University College
14 Old University College Hospital
15 Georgian Houses by Adam Brothers
16 Fitzroy Square
17 Communist Working Mens Club
18 Percy Street
19 Fitzroy Tavern

Tavistock
Square

Gordon
Square

10

11

12

Woburn
Square

9

SOAS

8

7

Russell Square

6

Keppel
St

Senate House

British Museum

Bedford
Square

5

Bloomsbury St

4

Gt Russell St

Bloomsbury
Square

Bury Place

2

1

Sicilian Av

Southampton Row

3

Bloomsbury Way

Stop 1

This was the first of the great squares of Bloomsbury to be laid out and dates back to 1661 under the patronage of the Earl of Southampton. His daughter married the Earl of Bedford who thus took over the estate and gave the area its names. Houses were built on three sides of the square with the oldest ones to your left, on the western side dating back to the 1660s, along which we now walk. Many people, famous in their time, lived here. We still remember John Radcliffe, benefactor of Oxford's Radcliffe infirmary (No.5) and Benjamin Disraeli (No.6).

Walk along the square to the north west corner with Great Russell Street and turn left. These houses were rebuilt by the great Regency architect John Nash. However, the development was not a success and Nash was declared bankrupt as a result. His debts weren't helped by the fact that he had just gone through a spectacular and costly divorce. His wife had attempted to pass off babies that she had purchased as her own with the father being named as John. She had then run off with a lover, the wonderfully named Charles Charles, and had borne a child with him. The gory details had enthralled London at the turn of the nineteenth century but hadn't done Nash's reputation much good.

Walk past Nash's houses then turn left down Bury Place. You walk past the wonderful book-shop and even better cafe of the London Review of Books; the little secluded square at the back can be very peaceful in summer.

Notice further on the Blue Plaque commemorating Bertrand Russell, the great twentieth century philosopher and scion of the Bedford family who lived here during the First World War.

Stop 2

It was here that he embarked on a passionate relationship with Lady Ottoline Morrell with whom he exchanged over 3,500 letters. While they were not core members of the Bloomsbury Group they were certainly on the periphery. Indeed Lady Ottoline had relationships with both Dora Carrington and Roger Fry who were certainly key participants in the group.

Walk to the main road, turn right and in a few metres you are standing outside one of London's great churches; St. George's, Bloomsbury.

Stop 3

This was designed by Nicholas Hawksmoor as part of the Queen Anne Fifty Churches Act, to spread the Church of England into the slums that bedevilled London in the early eighteenth century. Only twelve were built and Hawksmoor was responsible for six of them.

This one is truly remarkable. If you can, try and catch a glimpse of the tower. Its architecture is based on ancient monuments in Greece and Lebanon; around it are fighting unicorns and lions symbolising the end of the first Jacobite rising of 1715 and the whole thing is topped off with a statue of George I. It features in Hogarth's well known engraving 'Gin Lane'.

Inside, the church is unexpectedly beautiful, full of light given the sometimes gloomy surroundings. It was here that the funeral of the suffragette, Emily Davison, was held after she had thrown herself at the King's horse in the Derby of 1913.

Come out of the church and walk a short distance further west before turning right into Museum Street. This pedestrianised street leads straight to the main entrance of the British Museum and is full of interest. On your right Ruskin's Tea Rooms remind us that John Ruskin's work was published at No. 40 by Allen and Unwin as were the books of JRR Tolkien. In the same building was the HQ of the Men's League for Women's Suffrage which supported the suffragette cause before the First World War.

Stop 4

You arrive at the British Museum, one of the great cultural institutions of London and indeed the world. It was the very first public national museum and dates back to 1753 while the current building was built around 1850. Today it is the biggest visitor attraction in the UK with over five million visitors a year and can be very, very crowded.

Walk left down Great Russell Street and then right into Bloomsbury Street. Very soon you arrive at the south east corner of Bedford Square, one of the architectural highlights of our walk.

Stop 5

Bedford Square was built in 1780 and has survived almost unscathed over the last 250 years.

No. 44 on the west side of the square was home of Lady Ottoline Morrell when she and Bertrand Russell were engaged in their relationship while at no. 48, Bedford College was created in 1849, the first higher education college for women in Britain. Its students included George Elliot.

When you have almost circumnavigated the square, continue up Gower Street. There were a number of famous residents in this very short stretch. At No. 2, the suffragette Millicent Fawcett lived while at No. 7 there is a plaque commemorating the foundation of the Pre-Raphaelite Brotherhood in 1848. Lady Ottoline Morrell moved from Bedford Square to live at No. 10 where she had affairs with Dora Carrington and Roger Fry of the Bloomsbury set.

Walk through the entrance to Senate House on your right.

Stop 6

Senate House is London's first skyscraper. Built in 1937, it towers over Bloomsbury and its style is very redolent of the Soviet or Fascist architecture of the period. It is said that Hitler wanted to use it as the Nazi Party HQ when the conquest of Britain was complete. Today, it is the library of the University of London but during the Second World War it housed the Ministry of Information. Graham Greene worked here and used the setting in his novel 'The Ministry of Fear'.

More famously, it is said that George Orwell, who was also employed there, used it as the inspiration for the Ministry of Truth in his dyStopian novel '1984'. Orwell's boss was Brendan Bracken and some say his initials gave us Big Brother. What is true is that Orwell met his second wife Sonia Brownell at the Ministry who was employed as a censor there and she is believed to be the model for Julia, the lover of the novel's 'hero' Winston Smith.

Walk through Senate House to reach Russell Square.

Stop 7

Russell Square is the largest 'true' square in London. Lincolns Inn Fields, while larger, was never designed as a square but rather was gradually developed around common land.

Walk to your left, northwards along the side of the square.

Stop 8

When you reach the north west corner of Russell Square, note the plaque on the wall of the Faber building which commemorates the poet, T. S. Eliot, who worked there for forty years. What the plaque doesn't mention is that his first wife paraded outside the offices in the 1930s with a placard, denouncing Eliot for abandoning her. Virginia Woolf published the first edition of Eliot's most famous poem, 'The Wasteland', but famously turned down the opportunity to publish Ulysses by James Joyce.

Notice also the green hut on the corner of the square. This is an original cabman's shelter, set up in the 1870s to provide hot meals for cabbies. Only 13 are now left on the streets of London of the 61 originally built.

Walk through the passageway passing the entrance to SOAS in front of you into Woburn Square.

Stop 9

Woburn Square is the smallest square in Bloomsbury and was built by the great nineteenth century property developer, Thomas Cubitt. As you walk into the children's playground on your right is a sculpture of a Green Man. Beside it there is an extract from Virginia Woolf's novel 'The Waves', her most experimental novel, which inspired the statue.

Continue walking through the square noticing the little garden hut looking like a village pavilion and perhaps slightly incongruous in its urban surroundings. Turn right as you come out of the gardens and walk for a few hundred metres past the south side of Gordon Square into Tavistock Square.

Stop 10

Enter the square by the gate on the south side by the Tavistock Hotel. This hotel was built on the site of Virginia Woolf's last London house where she lived from 1924 to 1939 and where she wrote all her great works such as Orlando or Mrs Dalloway. Inside the square in the south west corner is a bust to Virginia. Walk through the square noting the statue of Gandhi and the memorials to the victims of Hiroshima. On the east side of the square by BMA
House is a plaque commemorating Charles Dickens who lived overlooking the square for the last ten years of his life.

Walk through the Square and then turn to your left down Endsleigh Place and very soon you enter Gordon Square.

Stop 11

Gordon Square, for many years, was the epicentre of the Bloomsbury Group and the place where its activities really began.

No. 46 Gordon Square can claim to be the most important house for the history of the Bloomsbury Group. It was here that Virginia and Vanessa first moved to Bloomsbury after the death of their father and where the meetings of the group on Thursday evenings began. Vanessa then lived here with her husband, Clive Bell, for ten years after Virginia moved out. It wasn't a happy marriage and both engaged in numerous affairs. When they separated the house was taken over by J. M. Keynes and the world famous economist lived here with his wife, the Russian ballerina Lydia Lopokova, till his death in 1946. Close by at No. 50 Vanessa Bell lived with her lover Duncan Grant after her marriage to Clive Bell broke down. When Clive returned to the family home Vanessa and Duncan moved a few houses up the square to No. 37. Here they had a child even though Grant had had many homosexual relationships up until this point.

At no, 51, Lytton Strachey lived in a strange ménage a trois with Dora Carrington and her husband Ralph Partridge. When Strachey died of cancer in 1932, Dora committed suicide at the age of 39. Further up the Square is Dora's original flat in the early 1920s, No. 41.

Walk through the garden across the square to the grand buildings on its south western side. At No.18 Graham Greene and Dorothy Glover lived together in an arrangement which partly inspired his novel 'The End of the Affair'. At the end of the nineteenth century, Sir Frederick Treves, the surgeon who rescued Joseph Merrick, the 'Elephant Man' lived in the same house.

Stop 12

There are two remarkable buildings in the south west corner of the square. The first is Dr Williams's Library, a neo-Jacobethan pile built in the mid nineteenth century, which is still in use and specialises in texts on English religious non-conformity.

Next to it is the extraordinary Church of Christ the King. This enormous building is a good example of Victorian mock-Gothic but was never fully completed. Today it hosts a number of Anglican groups and a small part of it is normally open to the public. It's well worth a quick visit.

Walk west into Byng Place and then along Torrington Place. Turn right into Gower Street and walk down it to the entrance of University College London.

Stop 13

Stop outside the grand entrance to University College London, the great intellectual bastion of Bloomsbury. It was created in 1826 as the first university in London and, along with Durham, the first to break the monopoly of Oxford and Cambridge. It was also the first university to

be open to students of all faiths or none and fifty years after its foundation became the first university to admit women on the same terms as men. Called by Thomas Arnold 'That godless institution on Gower Street', it is now one of the world's great universities.

Inside is one of the most extraordinary sights in London: the 'auto-icon' of Jeremy Bentham. He was one of the leading philosophers of the first half of the nineteenth century, known for his theory of 'utilitarianism' which posited as its rule for action the promotion of the greatest good for the greatest number. He was a keen reformer of prisons, schools, education and has been described as 'the spiritual founder' of UCL.

Bentham left instructions that on his death his body should be given for dissection and the remains preserved. Nearly 200 years later, he is still on display inside the university. To find him go into the university through the doors to the right of the main entrance, through the Japanese Garden, into the Student Union building where you'll find him in a glass cabinet.

The University has three remarkable museums: the Petrie Museum of Egyptian Archaeology, the Grant Museum of Zoology and its Art Museum. They are normally open between 1 and 5pm on weekdays and are well worth a visit.

Return back to the Gower Street entrance.

Stop 14

Opposite UCL is the old University College Hospital building built in flamboyant style in 1895. It's called the Cruciform as it has four wings designed to catch the light and breeze. In 1950, George Orwell died in Room 65 from TB shortly after marrying his second wife, Sonia Brownell, from his hospital bed.

Turn left down Grafton Way and after 200 metres cross Tottenham Court Road. You are now leaving Bloomsbury and entering Fitzrovia, an altogether less genteel, more bohemian area. Fitzrovia was, and still is, poorer and edgier than its more upmarket neighbour. Today it is dominated by the creative industries whether in the form of TV companies or architects. It is still much more 'lived in' than Bloomsbury with many more shops, restaurants and, especially, pubs. It also boasts a strong tradition of radical thought both native English and from abroad. This was a stomping ground of Karl Marx as well as anarchists from all over Europe.

Walk down Grafton Street.

Stop 15

On your right hand side the fine Georgian houses date from the 1780s and were designed by John and William Adam, brothers of the more famous Robert Adam.

Numbers 54, 56 and 58 have strong connections with the battles for South American independence from Spain in the first quarter of the nineteenth century. A plaque attests to Francisco de Miranda, hero of Venezuelan independence who stayed there and was visited by the splendidly named Bernardo O'Higgins, leader of Chilean independence and Simon Bolivar, hero of Bolivian liberation.

Continue into Fitzroy Square.

Stop 16

Fitzroy Square is, architecturally, a stunner. Its south and east sides were built by the great Scottish architect, Robert Adam in the 1790s.

The rest of the square was only finished forty years later. In the middle there is a fine garden with plenty of places to sit and admire the view.

There are a number of houses in the Square heavily associated with the Bloomsbury Set.

On the north side at No. 18, Clive Bell, Vanessa's estranged husband died in 1964. On the west side at No. 21, John Maynard Keynes lived with his lover Duncan Grant before Keynes married and Grant began his long relationship with Vanessa.

No. 29 has two plaques: the first to George Bernard Shaw who lived here in the 1890s and wrote such classics as 'Arms and the Man' and 'The Devil's Disciple' here. Ten years later, Virginia Woolf lived here before her marriage after decamping from Gordon Square. She continued to host the Thursday evening meetings of the Bloomsbury Set here.

On the south side, there is a plaque to the architect Robert Adam. At the same address lived Ford Madox Brown, the Pre Raphaelite painter. No. 33 was where Roger Fry, a key member of the Bloomsbury Set established his Omega workshop along with Vanessa Bell and Duncan Grant. They produced textiles, furniture and household objects all influenced by the artistic trends proliferating in Paris at the time. Roger Fry led the drive to popularise these new trends and it was said that he was 'incomparably the greatest influence on taste since Ruskin … In so far as taste can be changed by one man, it was changed by Roger Fry'. Whilst working as directors he had a passionate affair with Vanessa and was devastated when she went to live permanently with Duncan Grant.

Leave the Square at the south east corner down Fitzroy Street.

As you leave the square, notice the statue of Francisco de Miranda whose house we passed earlier.

No. 37 Fitzroy Street carries a proud literary history. It was the boyhood home of the author of 'The Ragged Trousered Philanthropists', Robert Tressell. A few years later, George Bernard Shaw lived here before moving to Fitzroy Square. Today, it is associated with another branch of fiction as it is the museum devoted to the Church of Scientology as it once was the church's London HQ; its founder L Ron Hubbard used to live nearby in the 1950s.

Carry on down Fitzroy Street until you reach Tottenham Street.

Fitzroy Street and its later continuation used to be at the heart of intellectual Bohemian and immigrant London. Among those who lived, met and worked on this street were dozens of Victorian painters such as Edward Burne-Jones, Paul Nash, James Whistler, and later Augustus John; anarchists like Louise Michel who fought in the Paris Commune or Martial Bourdin who died exploding a bomb in Greenwich; poets like Rupert Brooke, Wyndham Lewis, Ezra Pound and Dylan Thomas; or novelists like George Orwell. Alas, much of that has now disappeared, destroyed by the Blitz and then by unsympathetic planning as the great architectural and TV production firms moved in that now dominate the area.

Turn right into Tottenham Street.

Walk down to No. 49. This was the site of the Communist Working Men's Club. Marx and Engels were frequent visitors and Eleanor Marx, Karl's daughter, and William Morris also met here.

Retrace your steps to Goodge Place to see the modest mural that details some of the notable inhabitants of the area.

Stop 17

The figures portrayed include Virginia Woolf, George Bernard Shaw, Marie Stopes, Simon Bolivar and Olaudah Equiano who was a key figure in the abolition of slavery and also a member of the London Corresponding Society. The LCS was one of the earliest working class movements in Britain calling for the vote but was repressed by the government worried that the movement might try to emulate the French Revolution taking place across the channel.

Walk down Goodge Place pausing for a second outside No.11 where Arthur Seale another member of the LCS lived. Cross Goodge Street and walk down Charlotte Place in front of you and into Rathbone Street. You're now very much in the area made famous by the hard drinking bohemian pub culture of Fitzrovia before, during and after the Second World War.

You soon come to the Duke of York pub where Anthony Burgess and George Orwell often drank together. A bit further down you come to another of Orwell's pubs, the Newman Arms which apparently inspired the pub where Winston tried to meet the Proles in his novel '1984' as well as the pub in his earlier novel 'Keep the Aspidistra Flying'. In an upper window you'll see the portrait of a woman attempting to entice you in recording the fact that it was once a brothel. Next is the

Marquis of Granby which claims T.S. Eliot and Dylan Thomas amongst its clientele.

Carry on down to the Wheatsheaf pub which is where Dylan Thomas, George Orwell, Augustus John, Jacob Epstein and Nina Hamnett went to after they abandoned the Fitzroy Tavern after the Second World War once it became too well known.

Retrace your steps and on your right is the tree-lined Percy Street.

Turn into tree lined Percy Street, another historic street full of literary interest.

Stop 18

The street repays careful study but given that we are at the end of the walk and we've already left the best pubs behind a list of the most interesting houses may suffice. At No. 1, Wyndham Lewis and Ezra Pound celebrated the launch of the Vorticist movement in 1914. At No. 4 which stands out for its Art Nouveau tiling, a certain Alois Hitler stayed with his wife in 1910. She later claimed that Adolf, Alois's half-brother, came to visit them here. At No. 13 is the Elysee Greek Restaurant, London's first. George Orwell and Arthur Koestler ate moussaka together here. Orwell apparently loved the dish while Koestler hated it.

At the end of the street at No. 18 Sonia Brownell, Orwell's second wife was living when he met her. The flat was the inspiration for Winston and Julia's trysts in '1984'. Opposite Sonia and 150 years earlier, the first great English feminist, Mary Wollstonecraft, had lived with her newly born baby and had tried to commit suicide after her lover left her.

Retrace your steps into Charlotte Street and turning right you soon come to the Fitzroy Tavern.

Stop 19

This is the pub which gave the whole area its name. In the 1930s and 40s it was the centre of intellectual life with Augustus John, George Orwell and Dylan Thomas all regular drinkers here.

Finally

This is as good a place as any to end our walk although any of the other pubs or indeed the hundreds of restaurants in the area will revive you.

The closest stations are Goodge Street on the Northern Line or Tottenham Court Road on the Central or Northern Lines.

Twenty-first Century London

We have finally reached the modern city and what are we to make of it?

Well, it has certainly been transformed over the last few decades. Growing up in the fifties and sixties, for me, London was a grey and often gloomy place. While there were pockets of excitement in 'the swinging sixties' in Richmond, Chelsea and Soho, much of London was drab and indeed dirty.

London had been devastated by the Blitz and way into the fifties and even beyond there were bomb sites waiting to be redeveloped. When they were developed much of the architecture was not particularly memorable or inspiring. There were exceptions of course. The creation of the South Bank complex brought brutalism with its huge walls of rough concrete to the centre of London while the Barbican similarly divided opinion in the north. At least these were great public buildings that had the confidence of their style. All too often, however, the architecture of central London was either nondescript or actively disliked. Two examples from the sixties and seventies can illustrate this: Centre Point by Tottenham Court Road is often cited as an example of a purely speculative building completely out of scale with its surroundings. A second example is the Tower Hotel next to Tower Bridge, regularly voted the ugliest building in London and ruining the views of the river.

The great post war achievement was not in the big corporate buildings, rather it lay in the rehousing and slum clearance programmes of the fifties and sixties. For the first time most of the poorest Londoners had access to purpose built accommodation with private bathrooms, running hot water and adequate space as successive governments competed on their pledges to build more housing.

Economically, the last half of the twentieth century was also a time of great change in London. The manufacturing base of the city began to decline from the sixties onwards with the rise of globalisation and the export of production to cheaper areas of the world. The great industrial estates of north and west London gradually began to shrink. The closure of the docks in East London in the early seventies was a massive blow economically, condemning ten miles of the riverside and tens of thousands to unemployment. The population of London steadily dropped over the years as people moved away from what seemed to be a declining city. Partly as a result of these changes, there were also worrying signs politically. The rise of the racist right led to clashes on the streets unseen since the days of Mosley in the thirties.

By the late seventies there seemed little vision for London other than decline.

Things began to change in the 1980s. The liberalisation of the financial markets saw money flooding into London and the great international firms began to create new headquarters first in the City and then later around Canary Wharf. London's Docklands became one of the biggest regeneration projects in the world turning an unemployment hotspot into a new city where 130,000 people make their daily commute. For the first time in 300 years there was a concerted attempt to shift the focus of London from the west back towards the east; a long overdue rebalancing act. The arrival of a directly elected mayor gave London a stronger voice and a greater identity as a city brimming with self-confidence. The population of London began to grow rapidly at the end of the twentieth century from a low of 6.7 million in 1980 to 9.3 million in 2020, its biggest ever. It was a very different population too with over a third being born overseas and significant groups from Eastern Europe, the Mediterranean and from just about every continent in the world. Schools routinely report their children as speaking a hundred plus different languages in their homes.

Publicly the city glitters, at least in Central London. It is one of the great public cities of the world with renowned parks, open spaces and nearly 300 museums and art galleries. London generates more GDP than anywhere else in Britain with Greater London being home to a third of all the wealth in the United Kingdom. And this despite the financial crisis of 2008 and the impact of Brexit. Of course, that wealth is not shared equally. London is England's richest city but also its poorest and most unequal. Over 2 million Londoners today live in poverty, one of the highest rates of inequality in any western city. In particular, there is a crisis of housing where poorer people can no longer afford to live in central London boroughs. The introduction of 'right to buy', 'buy to rent' or 'buy to invest' and the failure of both the market and the state to build decent, cheap housing have all helped dry up the flow of affordable housing. The last twenty years have meant that those on low incomes now find it difficult if not impossible to get on the housing ladder.

However, there are signs of hope. London's public education system is outstanding with more disadvantaged students entering higher education than ever before and more than anywhere else in the country. Its transport system is world class and has been transformed over the last few decades with the introduction of new tube lines and cycle routes. Above all, there is still a sense of optimism and dynamism in London despite the difficulties of the last few years.

Perhaps the most visible symbol of the regeneration of London is its skyline. The architecture of London today is a far cry from the drabness of the post war period. London has grown upwards and today possesses a group of iconic buildings unsurpassed in Europe. Led by super-star architects like Richard Rogers and Norman Foster, areas of London such as the Docklands, Stratford and Wandsworth have been transformed. The change really started in the early 1980s when Richard Rogers was given the commission to design the new Lloyd's building. Its futurist design with services visible on the outside transformed the ambitions of British Architecture. By the time of the Millennium, the rebuilding of the City was in full swing and a series of highly distinctive buildings emerged often with public spaces on higher floors. So distinctive were they that they were given instantly recognisable nicknames: the Gherkin, the Cheesegrater, the Walkie Talkie and the Shard. Between them they have changed the look and feel of the centre of the City.

Walking London's modern architecture

On this walk, we will concentrate on London's modern architecture and how the City has been transformed over the last forty years. We will be contrasting the buildings of today with some of the classic landmarks of the City.

Walks starts at London Bridge Station and finishes at St Paul's.

Come out of London Bridge Station and make your way to the southern end of London Bridge on the corner by Tooley Street. There are multiple exits from the station but the bridge is sign-posted and pretty obvious.

See next page for the map of this walk...

Stop 1

Stand on London Bridge. Behind you rises the Shard, the tallest building in Britain, standing 309 metres over 95 floors. Designed by the Italian architect Renzo Piano, there were many criticisms before it was built but today it is generally seen as one of London's great modern buildings and a worthy addition to the London skyline. The modernity of the Shard is in marked contrast to Southwark Cathedral which can be seen just across the approach to London Bridge.

In front of you over the river is a wonderful panorama of the City of London, stretching from St. Paul's in the west, the Monument ahead of you to the Tower in the east. In particular, the great buildings of the new City are just in front of you: the 'Cheesegrater', the 'Walkie Talkie' and other ultra-modern buildings. It is these we will be walking to and exploring.

Walk over the bridge until you reach Monument Street on your right and walk towards the imposing sight of the Monument.

Stop 2

The column was designed by Christopher Wren and Robert Hooke and symbolises the rebirth of London after the devastating Great Fire of 1666. The Fire marked London's turning point from a medieval to a modern city and so is important in this review of London's architecture. In front of you is the engraving documenting the Fire's history by Caius Cibber. Remarkably he completed this panel while imprisoned in a debtors' prison. He tells the story of the Fire from its outbreak to the rebuilding of London, all under the benevolent gaze of Charles II. Where you're standing is much older than the Fire however; in fact originally it was the High Street of Roman London, linking the bridge with the Forum.

We will follow in the footsteps of the legionaries by turning left up Fish Street Hill. Turn right at Eastcheap, and then left up Philpot Lane and right into Fenchurch Street.

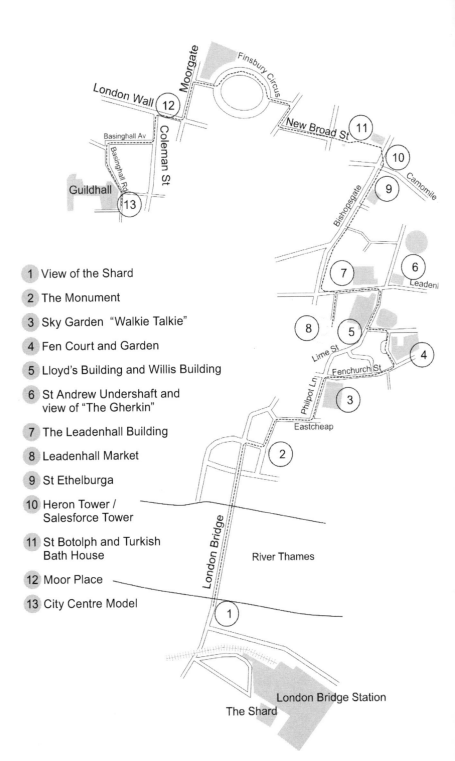

1. View of the Shard
2. The Monument
3. Sky Garden "Walkie Talkie"
4. Fen Court and Garden
5. Lloyd's Building and Willis Building
6. St Andrew Undershaft and view of "The Gherkin"
7. The Leadenhall Building
8. Leadenhall Market
9. St Ethelburga
10. Heron Tower / Salesforce Tower
11. St Botolph and Turkish Bath House
12. Moor Place
13. City Centre Model

Stop 3

You are now walking past 20 Fenchurch Street, aka the Walkie Talkie or Sky Garden. This is one of London's iconic twenty first century buildings. At the top of the building there is a beautiful garden with bars and restaurants. It's free and open to the public but you must pre-book. The building leapt to notoriety shortly after it opened when the sun's rays which were reflected from the building melted the interiors of cars parked below it. The windows had to be replaced at great cost.

Walk to your right down Fenchurch Street until you come to the entrance of 120 Fenchurch Street, the entrance to Fen Court.

Stop 4

While this has 'only' 15 stories it is surely one of the most spectacular new buildings in London. You enter through a vast atrium where there is an ever-changing art installation projected on the roof. Even better, there is free access to a beautiful garden suspended in mid-air. Well worth a visit at any time of the day, the public are welcome subject to space constraints.

Walk through the square and turn to your left.

Stop 5

In front of you, there is the iconic Lloyd's Building with its piping, heating and lifts all on the outside of the building, freeing the interior. It was the first of the new wave of modernist buildings in London at the end of the twentieth century. It was designed by Richard Rogers and opened in 1986.

Opposite Lloyd's Building there is also the remarkable Willis Building designed by Norman Foster in 2008 with its three overlapping towers.

Turn to your right up Lime Street to the corner with Leadenhall Street. There is a view in front of you which sums up the wide range of architecture you can see in the City.

Stop 6

St. Andrew Undershaft, a jewel of Tudor church building, is framed by the instantly recognisable 'Gherkin' or to give it its proper name: 30 St Mary Axe. This was designed by Norman Foster and opened in 2004.

In front of you and to the left is the site for what will become the City of London's highest building, 1 Undershaft, when built it will be topped only by the Shard. It's already been nicknamed the Trellis due to what will be its distinctive cross bracing.

Cross the road into the square opposite and then look back. On your left, you see yet another addition to the London skyscraper scene: The Scalpel.

Walk down Leadenhall Street towards Bishopsgate.

Stop 7

On your right you pass The Leadenhall Building, much better known as 'The Cheesegrater' because of its distinctive wedge shape. It was designed like this to protect the view of St Paul's from the east. If you're getting vertigo from all this height and want some architecture on a more human scale then turn down Whittington Avenue on your left and within a few metres you're in Leadenhall Market.

Stop 8

Leadenhall Market has a history spanning 2,000 years. The site is the old Roman forum which at its peak measured a square with sides of 160 metres, twice the size of Trafalgar Square. A medieval hall was built here in the fourteenth century with a roof of lead, hence the name. It became a market specialising in fresh meat but today is mainly about providing lunches and after work drinks for the city workers of the area. The current building dates from the 1880s and was made internationally famous by appearing as Diagon Alley in the Harry Potter films.

Retrace your steps back to Leadenhall Street and walk to the corner with Bishopsgate and turn right towards Liverpool Street. On your left is Tower 42. This used to be known as the Nat West Tower and was the first proper skyscraper in the City standing at 183 metres. From 1980 to 1991 it was the tallest building in the UK.

On your right you soon come to 22 Bishopsgate. This is another enormous skyscraper reaching 278 metres. It's had a difficult birth taking over twelve years to complete with changing owners and designs.

Stop 9

If by now you're feeling over-whelmed by corporate power and wealth and your neck is aching from always looking up then there's welcome relief as you pass on your right the tiny medieval church of St. Ethelburga. Badly damaged by the IRA Bishopsgate bomb in 1993, it has been rebuilt as a Centre for Peace and Reconciliation. The church is simple in the extreme and has a tiny hidden garden providing a haven of peace in the middle of the city.

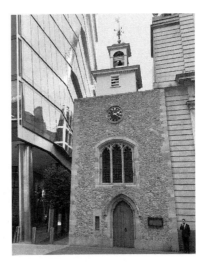

Keep walking up Bishopsgate to the corner of Camomile Street where two enormous buildings loom over you.

Stop 10

The first at 172 metres high is 100 Bishopsgate. It gives the illusion of being twisted as its base is a parallelogram but ends at the top as a rectangle.

Across Camomile Street at 110 Bishopsgate is Salesforce Tower, although most people know it by its previous name, Heron Tower. Currently (2020) it is the highest building in the City of London at 230 metres and its top floors are open to the public in the form of a cocktail ba r and restaurant offering spectacular views. In its atrium it has the largest privately owned aquarium in the UK with 1,200 fish swimming around in a 70,000 litre tank.

Cross Camomile Street and Bishopsgate to the diagonally opposite corner and continue to walk up Bishopsgate. Turn left down by the side of the church of St. Botolph.

Stop 11

St. Botolph was the patron saint of travellers before St. Christopher became popular in the middle ages and there were originally four churches with that name by the gates of London to welcome arrivals to the city. This one was rebuilt in the 1720s and witnessed the baptism of John Keats. It remains a handsome Georgian church with a beautiful church hall in the churchyard.

A few metres past the hall is a wonderful little late Victorian Turkish Bath house now used as a cocktail bar.

Carry on walking to cross Old Broad Street and continue down New Broad Street. Turn right at Blomfield Street and then left into Finsbury Circus. Walk round the Circus, currently being used as a Crossrail depot, to exit at the opposite side, noting the massive Lutyens' building on your right built for the Anglo-Persian Oil Company (now BP).

Turn left down Moorgate passing the Globe pub next door to which the poet, John Keats, was born. Turn right down London Wall.

Stop 12

In front of you is the dramatic curved roof line of Moor Place. This is another Norman Foster designed building completed in 2005.

We cross London Wall and walk down Coleman Street and then right down Basinghall Avenue and left into Basinghall Street.

Stop 13

We are coming to the end of the walk for No. 80 Basinghall Street hosts a wonderful exhibition on the architecture of the City. It includes an enormous model of the Square Mile where you can trace your route and identify all the new buildings we have walked past and those that we had to miss out. The City Centre is there to promote debate on the changing nature of London's built environment so if you are moved to comment on what you have seen on the walk about the past and future of the square mile, you've arrived at the right place.

Finally

For refreshments, the Guildhall Yard within a few steps of the City Centre has a Food Court at lunchtime. If you want to see more of how London has evolved over the centuries the Guildhall Art Gallery has some wonderful paintings of London and is well worth a visit.

Two thousand years of history

In this walk of not much more than two miles, we are going to cover 2,000 years of history and pick up many of the themes that we've covered in our previous walks. We also go south of the river for the first time. Here we will see a different aspect of London, less official, less law-abiding and full of illicit and disreputable pleasures.

South London has always been somewhat apart from north of the river. The original Roman settlement was on the north bank where the land was higher and drier. The south was the place of arrival with a few buildings defending the bridge and welcoming newcomers. It remained a swamp for centuries. So flat and low was it that the great Viking king Cnut (Canute in popular myth) found it possible to build a canal through the marshland so he could attack Saxon London from the west.

In the medieval period the monks of Bermondsey Abbey began embanking the south and draining the marshes to create agricultural land on the borders of the City. Gradually the settlement in the south grew. The Bishops of Winchester built a grand palace near London Bridge and the great church of St. Mary Overie (a corruption of over the river) which in the twentieth century became Southwark Cathedral.

Borough High Street was full of taverns and coaching inns which welcomed visitors and said goodbye to travellers including Chaucer's pilgrims setting off for Canterbury. Food came from Kent, the 'Garden of England' to be sold in Borough Market and processed in Bermondsey. For the best part of a thousand years, south London was dominated by food production. By the twentieth century, the major employers in the area included Peek Frean biscuits, Hartley's Jam and Sarson's Vinegar as well as many brewers. As a result, Bermondsey became known as the 'Kitchen of London'.

But the main industry for centuries on the South Bank was pleasure. South London has always lain outside the jurisdiction of the City so what was discouraged or illegal there might be welcomed on the other side of the Thames. Brothels flourished from the twelfth century onwards despite periodic crackdowns from the authorities. In the 1540s it was still being described as 'a naughty place'. By the time of Elizabeth I and James I the area was dominated by theatres offering the latest plays by Shakespeare, Ben Johnson and Christopher Marlowe as well as bear and bull baiting arenas.

The other industry was imprisonment. The Bishops of Winchester had set up the Clink, the oldest and most famous prison, around 1150 and prisoners languished there in awful conditions until it was destroyed in the Gordon Riots of 1780. Other prisons included Marshalsea, where Charles Dickens' father was imprisoned for debt and Horsemonger Gaol where Dickens witnessed a public execution and wrote to The Times protesting at the spectacle.

In Victorian times the area was dominated by noxious industries especially leather production which was concentrated in Bermondsey.

Outside of the main thoroughfares much of South London was racked by disease and poverty. Philanthropic efforts had some impact, notably Guy's Hospital and the work of Octavia Hill, Lord Shaftesbury and others.

The twenty first century saw a remarkable renaissance of the area. Borough Market is now a mecca for food lovers and fine restaurants abound in Bermondsey. The area is physically dominated by the Shard, Europe's tallest building and a symbol of London's capacity to continually reinvent itself.

This walk offers us London's history with a rough chronological accuracy.

We start with the Romans on the north bank of the river, re-discover the medieval guilds and London's most famous mayor. We then head over the river and find ourselves in Tudor and Jacobean times in London's infamous theatre district of the early seventeenth century. We walk where Shakespeare once performed and where Pepys and Samuel Johnson drank. We will see who ran the brothels of Bankside and find out what they did with their wealth and their victims. We then enter the eighteenth and nineteenth centuries (with a brief nod to Chaucer and his Canterbury pilgrims) as we find ourselves walking in the footsteps of Keats and Dickens and the philanthropy of Georgian England. We finally end in the shadow of the iconic building of the twenty first century but with a well-earned drink either in a building that dates back four hundred years or one that overlooks the whole of London.

Walking London's history

On this walk we are going to summarise all we have seen and learnt in a short walk through Central London and then across the river. At each stop I give an indication of the most significant period in that area's history.

Walk starts at Cannon Street Station and finishes at London Bridge Station. *This walk's map appears on the next page...*

Stop 1: Roman London

We start our walk at Cannon Street Station, today a main line station serving Kentish commuters but 2,000 years ago it was the site of the Roman Governor's Palace. It is hard to imagine now but this once boasted courtyards, gardens and fountains as well as offices from where Roman Britain was ruled.

Come out of the main station exit and cross Cannon Street. On your right you will see the London Stone, possibly the marker from which all distances in Roman Britain were measured. In medieval times it was the ceremonial stone on which solemn oaths were taken and officials appointed. It has always played an important role in London's consciousness. In Jack Cade's rebellion of 1450, according to Shakespeare, Cade struck the Stone and proclaimed himself Lord of the City. Since then the mythological status of the Stone has been assured and all sorts of stories have been developed about its history and significance.

Walk back to the crossroads of Cannon Street and Walbrook and, if you have not visited it already in the first walk of this book, turn right and in fifty metres enter the Temple of Mithras in the basement of the Bloomberg Building. It is the most spectacular and informative Roman site in London and its displays of the artefacts found on site are both accessible and comprehensive in scope.

Stop 2: Medieval London

Otherwise turn left down Dowgate Hill and Stop at the corner of Cloak Lane. In medieval times Dowgate Hill was the valley of the Walbrook and where it met the Thames the Hanseatic League, traders from the Baltic, had their headquarters in the great Stahl Yard, importing timber, jade and furs for the London market. On your right there are the remnants of that trade, for here are located the guild halls of the medieval livery companies of the Skinners, the Dyers and the

1 The London Stone

2 Livery Company Halls

3 St Michael Paternoster Royal

4 Globe Theatre

5 'Christopher Wren' house and Cardinal Cap Alley

6 Original site of Globe Theatre

7 The Anchor Bankside

8 Winchester Palace

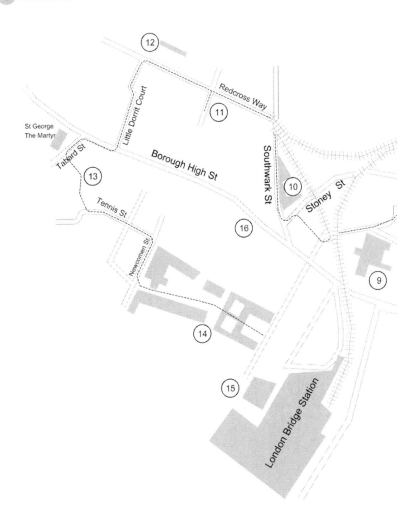

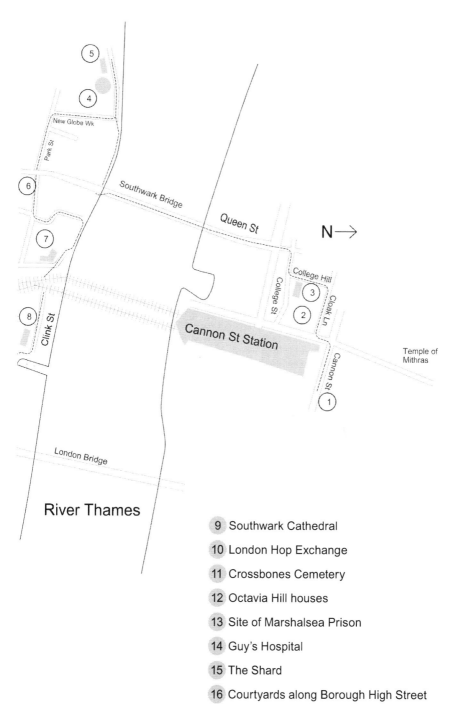

9 Southwark Cathedral

10 London Hop Exchange

11 Crossbones Cemetery

12 Octavia Hill houses

13 Site of Marshalsea Prison

14 Guy's Hospital

15 The Shard

16 Courtyards along Borough High Street

Tallow Chandlers. These three halls chart the journey of the bodies of sable, lynx and bears brought in from eastern Europe to end up on the backs of the rich. What was left of them ended up in Cannon Street, or Candlewick Street as it used to be called, their fat lighting London.

Turn down Cloak Lane. The name may conjure up images of nobles in flowing capes but in fact comes from the Latin Cloaca, and reminds us that this used to be a medieval sewer flowing into the Walbrook. Turn left into College Hill. This is Dick Whittington territory and you walk past the site of his house and arrive at his church, St Michael Paternoster Royal, in which he was buried.

Stop 3: Medieval London

The church's name comes in three parts; St. Michael is the arch-angel, Paternoster (our father) comes from the rosary beads that were made nearby and Royal probably derives from the French wine merchants who lived nearby and imported wine from La Reole near Bordeaux. The church has a long history, dating back to the twelfth century. It was rebuilt by Dick Whittington, destroyed in the Great Fire, rebuilt by Wren and, possibly Hawksmoor, and finally badly damaged in the Blitz. Dick Whittington was buried in the church but his grave has long since disappeared. Despite this, there are some interesting fittings in the church including a seventeenth century candelabra and a stained glass window depicting Dick Whittington, with

cat and streets paved with gold. Unfortunately, almost everything about Dick Whittington, the hero of Christmas pantos, is a myth. He wasn't a poor boy made good but instead was the son of a wealthy knight and became an important financier to Henry IV and V. It was said that he once threw an IOU from Henry V for the enormous sum of £60,000 into the fire at the Guildhall. He was renowned for his charitable works including the building of the church and, more prosaically, a monster public toilet with 64 seats overhanging the Thames.

Walk westwards up College Street, turn left down Queen Street, cross Upper Thames Street and walk over Southwark Bridge passing Vintners Hall, the old centre of the wine trade in London.

At the end of the Bridge go down the stairs on the right to emerge on to the Thames at Bankside.

Walk westwards towards the Globe Theatre.

Stop 4: Tudor London

For a thousand years South London has been a place of enter-tainment, of industry, of anything the City authorities didn't want. In particular in Tudor times it was a place for the theatre and other forms of diversion including, and especially, illicit sex.

The Globe Theatre is one of the great tourist attractions of London where, thanks to the efforts of the American Sam Wanamaker, you can see Shakespearean plays in authentic surroundings. For £5 you can stand in the pit for three hours in rain or sun while for £50 you can sit in even greater discomfort on backless, wooden seats. The building itself was constructed using the same materials and methods used in Shakespeare's day. It's in a great position overlooking the Thames although the actual site was a few hundred metres from its current spot. We'll visit the original site later in the walk.

Walk fifty metres beyond the theatre.

Stop 5: Tudor London

You notice a handsome house at No. 49 with a plaque claiming that ChriStopher Wren lived there during the building of St. Paul's Cathedral and that Catherine of Aragon, first wife of Henry VIII stayed there when she arrived in London.

Is it true? It would be wonderful if it was but in a fine book by Gillian Tindall, 'The House by the Thames' she traces the history of the house and its environs and shows that the house was built after the 1680s so, unfortunately, neither Catherine nor Wren could have lived there.

Alongside the house, is a narrow passage called Cardinal Cap Alley. This according to John Stow, chronicler of Tudor London, led to one of the more notorious brothels in sixteenth century London on land once owned by the Bishops of Winchester. They had been given the right to run the brothels of Southwark by Henry II and his Lord Chancellor (and future patron saint of London) Thomas a' Becket in 1156. The bishops grew rich on the profits of the brothels - we'll see the results later. Retrace your steps past the Globe and then turn right up New Globe Walk and then left into Park Street.

You pass Bear Gardens which is where bear and bull baiting took place in Shakespeare's day and then past Rose Alley, site of the first theatre built on Bankside in 1587. You can see what is left of the theatre on regular Saturday site visits.

As you cross under the bridge you will see on your right the remains of the original Globe Theatre.

Stop 6: Tudor London

Little is left of the theatre apart from a marker on the ground and some informative notice boards. The Globe was built in 1599 using materials from a previous Shakespearian theatre in Shoreditch. Shakespeare owned an eighth of the new theatre and he must have been mortified when it burnt down in 1613 after the roof caught fire from a cannon fired during one of his plays.

Keep walking along Park Street for 100 metres or so then turn left through a development, Red Lion Court, to reach the river bank again.

Stop 7: Seventeenth and Eighteenth Century

On your right is The Anchor one of the most famous pubs on the river for its historic literary connections. It was here that Samuel Pepys came on the first day of the Great Fire of London, 'to a little alehouse on Bankside' and saw 'one entire arch of fire from this to the other side of the bridge and in a bow up the hill for an arch of above a mile long: it made me weep to see it'. A hundred years later Samuel Johnson, a close friend of the family that owned the brewery to which the pub was attached, used to drink here. In 1773 a dinner was held here for Johnson's friends: Oliver Goldsmith, Joshua Reynolds, Edmund Burke and David Garrick. The pub even claims that Shakespeare drank here but that perhaps is speculative.

Walk under the railway arch into narrow Clink Street. You pass the Clink Museum, now a tourist attraction, built on the site of possibly the oldest prison in London, the present site dating back to the twelfth century. It was under the control of the Bishop of Winchester who had powers to imprison those within his jurisdiction, these included heretics, brothel keepers and debtors.

Stop 8: Medieval

In a hundred metres you come to the ruins of the great hall of the palace of the Bishop of Winchester. The building dates from the twelfth century and the ruins hint at the magnificence it must once have displayed. The bishops were senior clerics, immensely rich and powerful, third in the church's hierarchy, controlling lands from London to Winchester. The palace was the bishops' London seat.

Carry on past a replica of the Golden Hind, the ship on which Francis Drake circumnavigated the globe in 1580; it's good for children's parties but there are much more historic sites on this walk. In front of you is one of them: Southwark Cathedral, one of the greatest medieval churches of London.

Stop 9: Medieval

The church is one of the great glories of London. It dates from around 1100 although there has been a church here since Saxon times. It stands at the very entrance to London and would have been the first church to welcome travellers before they crossed the bridge into the City. To begin with it was a priory church and the monks ran a hospital alongside the church. This was the predecessor of St Thomas's Hospital, now located opposite parliament by Westminster Bridge. At the dissolution of the monasteries it became a parish church called St Saviour's, though many used its old name, St. Mary Overie until it became a cathedral in 1905. Inside, the church is very beautiful though it was heavily restored in the late Victorian period. There are monuments to John Harvard, a butcher from Borough who went on to found the famous University, the poet John Gower and William Shakespeare whose brother Edmond is buried in the Cathedral Choir.

Just to the south of the cathedral is Borough Market, one of the oldest and largest food markets in London. Its origins are lost in the mists of time. It was certainly there in the thirteenth century but the market claims to have been there since Saxon times. Today it operates under a fine Victorian roof and operates both a wholesale and retail function, the latter now concentrating on specialist foods. There is a very lively trade at lunchtimes in street food from around the world.

Wander through the market aiming for the corner of Stoney Street and Southwark Street.

Walk down Southwark Street a few metres and you will find the massive London Hop Exchange.

Stop 10: Victorian London

The Borough has been a centre for brewing for hundreds of years. Beer was indeed the daily drink of most Londoners as the water could not be trusted. Hops were brought from Kent as a key ingredient for brewers and in return many Londoners from south and east London would often spend their holidays in Kent hop-picking especially in the first half of the twentieth century.

The building in front of you is where hops were bought and sold and is normally open to visitors. The hops were kept in vast cellars below the building and samples would be inspected by the brewery representatives in the offices that line the inside of the building. Note the White Horse of Kent and the boughs of hops that decorate the iron work and facade.

Walk up Southwark Street and then turn left into Redcross Way, passing an old wine warehouse, The Boot and Flogger on your right. The name sounds highly dodgy but in fact are tools of the wine bottlers' trade.

You are walking, on your left, past one of the most extraordinary and moving places in London; the Crossbones cemetery. Turn left to find the entrance on Union Street.

Stop 11: Medieval

Crossbones Cemetery is an old medieval graveyard and the final resting place of the Winchester Geese, sex workers licensed by the Bishop to work in the brothels of Southwark. In medieval times, this was unconsecrated ground so the women were not allowed the sanctuary of the church even in death. Thousands of people were buried here until it closed in 1853 and the site was then built over. Rediscovered in the 1990s it has been turned into a garden of remembrance for the outcast dead; for all those rejected by respectable society. It is a wonderful secret place kept going by dedicated volunteers and constantly under threat of redevelopment.

Retrace your steps and keep walking up Redcross Way where there are a number of buildings originally dedicated to improving the lot of the poor in the area including St. Saviour's, a Christian Mission, and a 'Ragged School' run by Lord Shaftesbury.

Stop 12: Victorian London

You then arrive at the legacy of one of the most famous Victorian philanthropists, the founder of the National Trust, Octavia Hill. The small park, hall and cottages on your right were only a tiny part of her work to help London's poor and, in particular, to transform their housing. By the mid 1870s thousands of Londoners lived in small estates like this one which she had helped build and run. It was housing on a human scale with social facilities built into people's lives.

Continue walking up Redcross Way and turn left in to Little Dorrit Court. The name lets you know that we are entering Dickens' country. In his novel, Little Dorrit, Amy, our heroine, was brought up in the confines of the Marshalsea Debtors Prison, where Dickens' own father had been imprisoned and the prison is our next destination.

Turn right onto Borough High Street and then left into Tabard Street in front of the church of St. George the Martyr. The name Tabard Street reminds us that this is where pilgrims set off on pilgrimage to St Thomas a' Becket's tomb in Canterbury as immortalised in Chaucer's Canterbury Tales. The Tabard Inn where the pilgrims first meet is a few hundred metres away down Borough High Street. The church dates back to 1122 although the current building is from 1735. From the steps of this church, Henry V was welcomed back to London by its aldermen after the Battle of Agincourt in 1415.

Walk through the churchyard to your left to the gate in the wall. Go through it and turn to your right.

Stop 13: Georgian London

This is the only remaining part of the Marshalsea Prison where John Dickens, the father of Charles was imprisoned for debt. Charles never forgot the indignity and hardship that this caused him and his family. Turn right down the path where a plaque commemorates John Dickens' imprisonment.

Turn left into Tennis Street and right into Newcomen Street and then turn left into the grounds of Guy's Hospital.

Stop 14: Georgian London

Guy's Hospital was a testament to the growing philanthropy of the eighteenth century. It was founded by Thomas Guy for the 'incurables' discharged from nearby St Thomas' hospital. Walk straight through the grounds passing a plaque to Ludwig Wittgenstein, the great Austrian philosopher who worked, incognito, as a hospital porter during World War II and nearby a statue of John Keats, who trained at Guy's, placed in an alcove taken from old London Bridge.

Continuing further into the hospital you come to the original part of the hospital with on your left a beautiful eighteenth century chapel which is normally open to the public. It contains some fine Victorian murals in the Arts and Crafts style.

Walk out of the Hospital and turn left along Saint Thomas Street. On your left notice the plaque to John Keats who lived at no. 24 while training as an assistant surgeon. On the other side of the street you pass the Old Operating Theatre which dates back to the early nine-teenth century. Well worth a visit if only to feel thankful we live in an age with anaesthetics!

All the while we have been walking in the shadow of the Shard which towers 300 metres above us, the tallest building in the UK.

At this the end of the series of walks, I offer you the choice of two final Stops and a choice between two different visions of London:

Stop 15: Twenty-first Century

Walk back along St Thomas Street to the entrance to one of the Shard's six restaurants or to the viewing gallery on the very top of the building. Both choices are expensive but the lower floors can give you an even better view of London than the topmost floors. What the Shard gives you is an unparalleled overview of this magnificent city with views stretching 40 miles whilst standing in a symbol of the progressive rest-lessness that drives London forward.

OR

Stop 16: Tudor to today

Continue walking along St. Thomas Street and turn left along Borough High Street. Walk past the alleys on your left which used to house coaching inns where travellers to and from Canterbury and the Channel coast would start or finish their journeys. The fourth alley on your left is Talbot Yard where the Tabard Inn once stood, immortalised as the starting point of the pilgrims in the Canterbury Tales. We stop at the third alleyway for this holds the only surviving coaching inn in central London, the George. Now a National Trust property it reminds us what a traditional inn would have looked like in the seventeenth century. Dickens drank here and the shape with its galleries (which used to extend round three sides) could have been used to put on plays, an arrangement that Shakespeare would have been used to. The George epitomises London in its historic continuity; a city which can trace its history through the times of Dickens, Shakespeare and Chaucer and yet still be packed out on a Friday night with the latest generation of Londoners.

It's for you to decide with which London you wish to finish.

Printed in Great Britain
by Amazon